About the Author

Priscilla Mphanza Kandira lives in Lusaka, Zambia, in the Chelstone suburb. This is her second book based on actual experiences in her life. Some experiences she believes are mysterious and supposes you will find intriguing to read about. She believes God always inspires her art of writing.

Silent Mysteries

Priscilla Mphanza Kandira

Silent Mysteries

Olympia Publishers
London

www.olympiapublishers.com
OLYMPIA PAPERBACK EDITION

Copyright © Priscilla Mphanza Kandira 2023

The right of Priscilla Mphanza Kandira to be identified as author of this work has been asserted in accordance with sections 77 and 78 of the Copyright, Designs and Patents Act 1988.

All Rights Reserved

No reproduction, copy or transmission of this publication
may be made without written permission.
No paragraph of this publication may be reproduced,
copied or transmitted save with the written permission of the publisher,
or in accordance with the provisions
of the Copyright Act 1956 (as amended).

Any person who commits any unauthorised act in relation to this publication may be liable to criminal prosecution and civil claims for damage.

A CIP catalogue record for this title is
available from the British Library.

ISBN: 978-1-80074-864-4

This is a work of fiction.
Names, characters, places and incidents originate from the writer's imagination. Any resemblance to actual persons, living or dead, is purely coincidental.

First Published in 2023

Olympia Publishers
Tallis House
2 Tallis Street
London
EC4Y 0AB

Printed in Great Britain

Dedication

I dedicate this book to my loving husband, Paggie Paradzai Kandira, for the strong and blessed bond that we share. God was with us all the way.

Acknowledgements

Heartfelt thanks to my husband, Paggie Kandira, my father-in-law, Mr. Richard Tozivepi Kandira, and Agnes Mphanza and family for allowing me to share some of our life experiences. I pray it will be a lesson to someone who will find sense in this book. I also believe my children, Tinashe, Rumbidzai, Tozivepi, Simbarashe and Kudakwashe, and family generations to come will read about this and learn about the experiences of their parents and grandparents or great grandparents. May the Almighty God continue to bless our lives. Amen.

Chapter 1

The room was in silence except for his heavy footsteps as he paced about in anxiety. He stood arms akimbo for a while, and then muttered to himself the contents of his thoughts.

"I'll get it. I'll get that throne to myself." Itai went on, "By the time we are burying Runako, I should win all the support from my kindred to be crowned king."

He peered out of the window but could not get a clear view as the nimbus clouds were still heavy, creating a dark and foggy atmosphere. He was now standing in the doorway, looking in the direction of the women who busied themselves with various chores.

"Shamiso! Shamiso!" Itai called out to his wife.

"Baba! I'll be there in a minute," she responded quickly, coming from a small hut that acted as a cooking place. It was full of women and an overflow had formed outside as they prepared food for the mourners. It had rained heavily that morning and the place was wet with pools of water in some areas. Some villagers believed that it was a sign of anger from the ancestors over the manner in which the king had passed. That whoever had a hand in his death would be struck with lightning and die.

"Get here quickly. I've very important news to share with you." He was standing in the doorway awkwardly.

Shamiso quickly made her way, as she knew well how Itai didn't like to be kept waiting. He could be rough at times and very impatient.

"My apologies, dear husband. What bothers you this morning that you've to shout out loud like that with your people within hearing distance? Your kindred worried and wondered desperately."

"Let them worry. I don't care. *Ehe*, what I want to tell you, my wife, is that I've come up with a plan to supplant Fadzai for the throne. I'll grab it from him no matter what I've to do. However, you've to agree to my plan."

"What plan, my husband? I hope it's nothing dangerous." She was concerned.

"No, no, no, it's not anything like you're thinking. I just need you to allow me to marry Maita, you know, she's our gateway to the throne." He delivered the message as though it was the best news ever. There was a moment of silence before Shamiso's outburst. She was suffocating with the news while Itai looked calm but desperately expectant of her reaction. He knew with that kind of news, anything was expected.

"What? What did you say? You wicked man! Must you always have your wicked way. I had always suspected that you were interested in your brother's wife, you devil!" Shamiso quivered with fury. Her stomach roared and cramped like someone about to advance into diarrhoea. She looked at him with so much anger Itai thought she was going to strike him.

In her late thirties, Maita was spectacularly beautiful with a heavy, tantalizing hip. Of medium height, she was so light as to suggest mixed race pedigree. Most men in the village presented themselves to be her suitors, but Runako was the lucky one. After marrying Maita, Runako was constantly looking out for her as even his own cousins eyed her. Itai was one of the most mischievously dangerous, preying on Maita and looking for an opportunity to convince her to be intimate with him.

After Itai married Shamiso, it was obvious Itai still had not gotten over Maita, and his abhorrence for Runako was overwhelmingly treacherous. He was very much obsessed with Maita, and he could practically do anything. Shamiso was not as beautiful as Maita. She was short, plump with a flat figure and floppy breasts made even worse from childbearing. Itai married her at the recommendation of his parents, to please them. She came from a good family. Itai's parents had always monitored him for fear that he would do something reckless, concerning Maita, and Runako was ready to use the throne to fix him.

"Shamiso, lower your voice," Itai warned in an undertone.

"Oh, so now I should lower my voice; after all, you didn't care when you were on top of your voice shouting out my name. We've not concluded burial rites for your brother, and you're already planning to marry his wife. You're very iniquitous."

"Anyway, coming to think of it, I'm even considerate to let you know in advance because, you know, it's our custom to marry more than one wife. If you don't want to stay, you're free to leave. I'll not allow you to ruin my plan to rule over this kingdom. Never!"

Shamiso left Itai's presence in a rage that was so visible to everyone outside.

"What's the matter now?" Dumisani, Shamiso's son, whispered to Senzeni, his younger sister. He was seated on a lazy back chair, tossing some stones in his hand.

"Mother looks very angry. I've not seen her like that in a long time and particularly that she didn't mind the people out here. This must be very serious." Dumisani cleared his throat, trying to project his voice that was muffled by his sitting posture. He turned to look down at his sister, who also played with some stones. She sat crouched on the ground such that her chin rested on her knees.

"I smell a rat here, and it's not small," Senzeni added. "I'll go and persuade Mother to tell me what's cooking."

"Don't go making those jokes of yours like you're doing right now and asking stupid questions. In the state she's in, you'll receive a very good beating. Be serious for once in your life," Dumisani lectured his sister.

Senzeni was a tall slender, dark-skinned girl, seventeen years of age with an intelligent mind. Her slenderness made people in the village mock her and generally take no notice of her. She was fairly attractive, especially when she smiled, revealing her ivory white teeth that were evenly arranged except for one tooth that grew on top of the right canine. However, it didn't spoil her beautiful smile. Her father especially liked her most because of her intellect. She was his secret adviser and emissary in the village. Dumisani, on the other hand, was a big warrior-type young man, built and about 1.9 metres. Unlike his father, he was a hunter all his life taking after his grandfather, who took him on most of his hunting sprees. No wonder he left him all his hunting tools just before he died. However, his father, Itai, had always been an opportunist, taking advantage of his royal bloodline.

"I hear you, brother. This definitely is no time to joke. This is a bomb waiting to detonate; I can sense it," Senzeni concluded.

"Hashi, you with your colloquial English, get out of here already! What's wrong with you?" said Dumisani.

"Okay, brother, I hear you. I'm gone already." Senzeni ran past a group of women seated on a reed mat. A few of them were busy pounding maize into a flour for preparing nshima. Others were busy brewing beer for drinking at the funeral, as was customary when an elderly member was deceased.

Shamiso went behind the last hut away from the others and sat crying unbeknownst to anyone. Senzeni went around the huts in her search and caught up with her.

"Mother, what's the matter? Why are you crying?"

"It's your father. He's already planning to marry your aunty before we could even conclude your uncle's funeral."

"What did you say, ma? What's Father planning? Is he out of his mind? He's a nincompoop." Senzeni suddenly was even more furious than her mother.

"Mother, I need to confront Father for this! He can't be serious. He wants us to be calling our cousins brothers; no way! This is a disgrace. He's very selfish, only thinking about himself and not the happiness of others. And how does he think you're feeling right now, *hee*? If he does that, I'll run away to a place you won't find me," Senzeni hollered insults about her father.

"Don't say that, my daughter. Don't speak to him about that right now. It seems he has his mind made up. You'll only cause him to be angry with you. Leave it to me. It's between your father and me," Shamiso told her.

"And what was his reasoning to commit such an abominable thing?" she questioned.

"He wants to be King instead of Fadzai, your cousin."

"You mean Fadzai is supposed to be crowned king after his father?"

"Yes, Senzeni, we follow a patrilineal culture, meaning he's next in line, and your father is keen to take it away from him."

"But he's too young, Mother, and hasn't got a house of his own,"

"My daughter, it's possible for him to be crowned king."

Fadzai was born into a family of three boys. Tall, light-skinned and of a good build. He resembled the stature of his father Runako and was very kind-hearted. He was loved by his people, just like Runako. Fadzai's father passed away mysteriously in his sleep.

"You can't believe what Mother just told me," Senzeni began to speak as she joined her brother.

"Yes, don't waste my time if it's nonsense. I'm busy tying my catapults so I can get a kill for lunch." He cut in snappily while pulling on the strings to test them.

"You'll not even want to go in the bush when you hear what I've got to tell you. Let's go someplace private to discuss."

"Senzeni, this better be good now!"

"Let's go. It's news of the century," Senzeni assured.

The grounds of the palace were within a fence made from sticks and grass thatched around it. It was on the east side of the road on a hilly place overlooking the village on the other side. There were several small huts behind the palace where some family members and palace workers lived. Senzeni and Dumisani found one of the huts that was in a secluded place, away from the others. In whispers, Senzeni spoke to Dumisani.

"Brother, do you know that your cousin Fadzai, the one who takes all the women that you love, will soon be your king?"

"What! Say that again?" Dumisani gasped in shock.

"Fadzai is going to be your master and you the slave. How about that?"

"You're kidding me, sister. But he's young? I can't be subject to Fadzai, no way. We've always competed in many things, and I outsmarted him in most of them."

"Don't kid yourself, brother. Fadzai has always been better than you."

"Okay, okay, but I am also smart," he delivered a confident glance at his sister as she made a face in her indifference.

"Whatever, brother, suit yourself. However, it's true about Fadzai. And the reason why Mother was so upset is because Father wants to marry Aunty Maita to take the throne away from Fadzai." Senzeni spoke with a demeanour that began to change from mockery of his brother to anger.

"No! No way am I going to allow Fadzai to be king," Dumisani demanded

"What are you going to do about it?"

"We are going to convince Mother to agree to Father's plan to marry Aunty for the throne," Dumisani suggested.

"You mean you're ready to allow Fadzai, Kumbirai and Tamuka to be your brothers for this?" She was disgusted.

"Look, Senzeni, life will be much easier for us, and we shall command respect. And this will keep Fadzai in check and also create a chance for me in the future to be crowned king. Moreover, Fadzai will not always have his way on us." Dumisani concluded with a sardonic smile on his face.

"Having his way on you, not me. I feel this is not right. You're just being selfish like Father," she retorted.

"Okay, sister, but we've to act together so that our plan works."

"But I'm not as enthusiastic as you are in this matter, and I don't see why my non-participation can jeopardise your plan. So I'm suggesting you go it alone."

"That's true about your enthusiasm, but teamwork will get us the result we require. Please don't sabotage my plan." He was exasperated.

Senzeni rolled her eyes at Dumisani in disgust.

Dumisani announced his presence and entered his father's chambers. He'd just stopped inside the door and looked around for a place to sit as his father extended a greeting.

"Father, I heard from Mother that you want to marry Aunty Maita. Is that true?" Dumisani spoke with a steady voice.

"Son, I know you may not like the idea, but I'm just trying to secure your future and that of your sister. I need to lay my hands on this opportunity because it'll never come again," Itai emphasised.

"Father, I understand you," Dumisani assured.

"You understand?" Itai's face ignited in surprise.

"Yes, Father. We cannot allow Fadzai to become king while you are there." He repositioned himself to sit closer to his father.

"Yes, son. After all, he's only eighteen and not yet married." Itai put up his argument with confidence.

"That's not an issue, Father." Dumisani continued to assure him.

"But your mother is who we are supposed to worry about. She's against the idea so much she's not even speaking to me. She may decide to leave if I insist." Itai worried.

"Don't worry, Father, I shall talk to Mother and she will come around. Just plan on how you're going to break that news to your family. Right now, I need to go and see Mother." Dumisani rose to take his leave.

"Your mother can be very stubborn, you know. All the best in convincing her son."

"Put it this way, Father. It's a simple and easy job to do."

"Mother, may I have a word with you in private?" Dumisani walked vigorously and excused himself to the women seated with Shamiso.

In private, Dumisani began speaking, "Mother, Senzeni told me about Father's plan to marry Aunty Maita so that he can be king."

"Yes, Dumi. I don't think I'm ready to put up with this evil act. As soon as the funeral is over, I'm leaving for my father's house."

"No, Mother. Look, Father's intentions are good for all of us. He wants us to have an easy life. It's good for you as well. After all, you'll be the senior wife, making all the decisions. Think about it, Mother. The entire kingdom will respect you and shower you with gifts. You'll have anything that you want in the kingdom and live in the palace, which you didn't enjoy before. Think about this, Mother, and think about us as well. What's good for us," he begged.

As the evening dawned that day, the sounds of drums and people dancing under a well-lit moon drew a crowd. Villagers mourned their king with dances and drank the local brews. They stayed awake till morning as they prepared to put Runako to rest. He was buried the following morning in the field behind the palace that September 1967. The following day, the family gathered to conclude the funeral with a meeting attended by family members and elders of the village.

Tanyaradzwa, one of the elders, rose to speak.

"Fellow mourners, we are gathered here to converse about how we intend to drive this kingdom forward after the death of our king. I want to make it clear that our king died a very suspicious death but we need to proceed with putting in place a successor. According to our custom, the first son Fadzai should be crowned our next king. Any objections to that?" His eyes hovered around to focus on anyone who wanted to speak. "Nobody is saying anything. I rest my case for now."

"Excuse me, elders." Itai put up his hand to speak in a haste. "Seeing that I remain the only brother of Runako and he leaves behind a wife and three children, I'd like to marry my brother's wife and carry on his legacy. Especially that Fadzai is not mature enough and he's not yet married, therefore, cannot become king." He addressed the crowd.

There were murmurings among the group gathered for the meeting.

"How does he want to marry his brother's wife? What about his own?" the crowd inquired among themselves.

"What's that you're saying, Uncle! Marry my mother? He was your brother? What's the meaning of this?" Fadzai rose with so much force that he was restrained by the men seated close to him.

Another elder, a relative of Itai, rose to speak.

"I see nothing wrong with what Itai has proposed. It's our custom to take over our brother's wives. She's his wife as well. He will take care of Runako's family and the throne. Fadzai, you're still too young to understand this and sit on the throne."

Further murmuring and grumbling was heard.

"Is anyone objecting to what has been proposed here?" Tanyaradzwa spoke.

Fadzai almost rose to speak again, but he was further restrained by the men.

"Don't rush to challenge your uncle; you may find yourself in a dangerous situation." The men spoke in whispers to him. "Remember, Tanyaradzwa alleged that your father died under suspicious circumstances. Hold yourself and watch what's happening."

"Silence means we all agree to Itai's enthroning," Tanyaradzwa said.

"Elders shall prepare to enthrone him in the next two weeks. We may disperse."

Fadzai left the meeting confused and enraged. "How can Uncle possibly think of doing such a horrible thing? Marry my mother? I need to speak to him one on one. He needs to explain this."

"How can you announce your intention to marry me at the meeting without even telling me? You made a foolish spectacle of me in front of all those gathered as if we had it all planned," Maita grumbled to Itai in a contemptuous tone of voice that took him by surprise.

"See, my dear, I've good plans for us, and moreover, I adore you very much. You know I loved you even when my brother was still alive. I was supposed to marry you instead of him. I'll make sure you've everything you need. Look, you're growing older and no one will marry you. At least you'll still have a chance to enjoy the position as queen even after Runako's death. I can guarantee you that."

"What about your wife? She has been like a sister to me. I can't do a preposterous thing like that to her."

"C'mon, I'll handle her, and it's good. She already knows I'm taking you for a wife."

"My husband has just been buried and you're talking about marriage?"

"It's for your own good, and the people need a king remember?" For a moment, he almost pulled her to himself to embrace her, but she pushed his hands away.

"But who is stopping you from becoming a king? You can become one without me."

"You know it's a way of having you, Maita, and making sure

that no one else has you. Think about it."

"Give me some time to think this over," Maita retorted.

Fadzai entered the cooking house and found his mother preparing supper. Because of his anger, the strong smell of spicy herbs mixed with smoke that came from inside the house caused him to feel nauseated.

"Where have you been, my son? I was worried sick about you. You left the meeting in a rage this morning and were nowhere to be seen?" Maita complained.

"I needed time to think, Mother, before coming to speak to you. You heard what Uncle said at the meeting about you. What do you say about that, Mother?" He was leaning on the bamboo cupboard, looking directly at his mother, who was now standing about a meter from him. His anger caused him to breathe fast and noisily.

"It's very difficult for me to return to my people, son. I've advanced in age already."

"Wait, Mother! So, you want to be married to him? What about us? You don't care about us?"

"It's not that, my son. I want you to continue enjoying the position you have always held. I don't think you can manage the throne at your age. I'm actually sacrificing for you."

"Mother, you don't need to sacrifice for us. Do what's right. From what I'm getting hearing you talk right now, you seem to have already made up your mind. I was about to speak to Uncle, but I believe there's no need for that." Fadzai bemoaned. He hit the cupboard, and cups hit each other, tumbling down to the ground, breaking as he began to walk out of the house in a fit of rage. His unmistakable rage was evidenced by the way he slammed at these items and sealed it with the slamming of the door on his exit.

"Fadzai! Fadzai, my son," his mother called out.

After the death of his father, Fadzai left the palace and moved in with his grandmother.

"Son, what are you going to do with these cattle?" Tinashe inquired.

"I'll tend to them myself. They can't be shepherded by anyone they don't know. They won't move unless I order them."

"But they're trouble, especially during the night. They break open the kraal and walk about in people's fields."

"Don't worry, Grandma; I'll be sleeping with them in the kraal. It's like they miss Father's presence."

"No, my son. How can a normal human being sleep with cattle? The kraal is dirty and smelly. I can't allow you to do that."

"Grandma, if I don't do it, we will have a lot of damages to pay, or else we sell all of them."

"But we can't sell all the cattle just now. It'll look like we are looting Runako's property. There'll be trouble with Itai."

"Yes, Grandma, let's wait. Let me be sleeping with them."

"See, my son, what the death of your father has caused you, so much suffering," she cried.

"It's all right, Grandma."

"Okay, okay, you can go ahead and sleep with them, but only for a few weeks. We've got to find a solution to this." Tinashe reluctantly agreed.

"We've managed to convince Mother to stay. Now what do we do with Fadzai? What happens if he decides to marry? Remember, he's eighteen years and that is possible. What if the elders say Father will only act as concierge for the throne?" Senzeni asked Dumisani.

"I've another solution for that."

"And what's that exactly?" Senzeni inquired.

"Hold on. I'll break it down for you."

Chapter 2

Senzeni and Dumisani stood at the entrance of a small dark hut with only a small opening that let in a gleam of light discernible from the outside. A dirty red cloth which drooped on it for a curtain was drawn to the side. It was a shrine for a *n'anga*, a village witch doctor. This was six months after Itai was crowned king. They heard a voice but didn't see the orator.

"Take off your shoes, leave them by the door, enter and sit down."

The two siblings hesitantly did as they were instructed. He led the way into this dim shackle of evil spirit filled sphere. The smell coming out of it was that of death, rotten human flesh. They were so flustered it showed in their actions. Fidgeted a lot and scanned around in astonishment of the so many idols that were lined up on a raised platform which stood for a table. Some had fresh blood coming out of their heads and others from their mouths. Green flies made a buzzing noise, killing the silence in the small room as they circled and settled back on the idols. Strange voodoo dolls hung on the walls with engravings on them.

"Dumisani, I don't think this is a good idea. I'm beginning to have this bad feeling down in my stomach. I'm going to throw up." Senzeni whispered her complaint to her brother.

"Shut up! We are already here. Let's do what we need to do and get out of here." Dumisani snapped in an undertone.

"What brings you here?" The voice thundered again, without a figure.

"We're here because we want you to help us kill our cousin Fadzai." Dumisani stammered some words out of his dry mouth while they looked around in fear.

"If you had the courage to come here, why didn't you do the killing yourselves?" roared the voice.

Senzeni nudged her brother with her elbow, "I knew we shouldn't have come here!" She panted as if coming from a jog. "We better leave this place now." She further protested.

He nudged her back in disagreement as he looked at her from the arch of his eye.

"All right," said the voice. "Bring me any of his clothes and his hair. I'll do the job. Give me two weeks. However, you need to do the following. Bring a goat and five hundred Rhodesian dollars as payment. Get a chicken, slaughter it, and then pour its blood at Fadzai's doorstep so that when he crosses it, I can connect him to this altar, you hear me?"

"Yes, we hear you," said Dumisani.

"Let's get moving Dumisani. I don't like this." Senzeni was almost crying out of fear.

When they left the shrine, they ran quickly through the thick bushes while Dumisani led the way. They came to a less bushy area and Senzeni gained some courage to speak, "Stick to the route we are familiar with; don't go another way or they'll never find us." After a few kilometres, Senzeni bemoaned as she took hold of her brother's hand:

"We need to rest." She stooped over, putting her hands on her knees. "I can't go on. My heart is thumping hard against my chest. It wants to rip it."

"Okay, let's sit over there." He pointed to a tree trunk that lay cut on the ground.

"Why're we doing this brother? We don't need to kill Fadzai.

Our father has already been crowned king. Why can't we leave him alone?" she waded off grass as she made her way to sit on the tree trunk.

"When he grows up, he may want to get the throne back," Dumisani replied.

"So what? We will have profited anyway!" Senzeni lashed at her brother.

"We need to finish what we've started," Dumisani retorted.

"I know it's now about your egotistic interest. You want to settle some scores hee! count me out." Senzeni bawled with anger as she lifted herself to her feet and hurriedly started off.

Dumisani remained in shocked realization. Horror gripped him, and a shiver rippled down his entire body when he thought of the gravity of their malevolent actions.

"Wait up! Senzeni. Wait for me!" he shouted to her.

"I can't believe what I'm hearing. What did you say again?"

"Dumisani and Senzeni visited a shrine to plot your grandson Fadzai's death," Rumbidzai narrated to her elder sister Tinashe.

"I happen to be a good friend of Nkongono, the *n'anga* of the village shrine. I told him to spare the young man, but it's just a matter of time and they may catch up with him.

"It's because I know him that he has delayed the process, hoping the two abandon it. If they don't, they'll want to push for it or see another shrine priest for results."

"I need to protect my grandson from these scavengers. Just because Itai is born from the other home from my Runako, they want to kill his son? I need to warn him. I never had problems with his mother, but now where is this hatred coming from?" The anger was now very vivid in Tinashe's voice. "I must act fast."

Tinashe was amazed when she discovered what horrifying scheme Fadzai's cousins were planning. Seeing that there was no relative to keep him in Zimbabwe away from the kingdom, Tinashe told Fadzai to cross over to Zambia and look for a long-lost relative of his father.

"Fadzai, my son, I'm too old and have nothing to offer you. See, your mother is now married to your uncle, and she's in his territory. She can't possibly see what's happening around her. I'll not allow that this throne be the reason for your suffering and death," Tinashe spoke amid sobs.

"In the name of your dead father Runako, run as fast as your legs can take you. Leave here and look for your uncle. I pray that God will be on your side and I bless you my son."

Fadzai spoke with fear and disbelief. "Where do I go, grandmother? I've never been out of this village let alone Zambia!"

"My grandson Fadzai, it's better that I just hear you never made it to Zambia than see you die at the hands of your own relatives; suffering from an incurable disease or die mysteriously like your father," Tinashe spoke while averting Fadzai's gaze to avoid seeing the terror in his eyes.

"If you make it where you're going and you hear I've gone to join your father and my ancestors, never return to this village. Stay in Zambia and raise your family there. The people you'll find there will be your family. Treat them well and they'll return the gesture. Here my son, receive this small bag of mealie meal, some dried fruits and vegetables to eat on your way. You'll use this money to pay for your fares. Don't tell your uncle, let alone your cousins that you're leaving. Just go quietly my son."

Fadzai thought about what his grandmother told him. He

later called his young brother.

"Kumbirai, I need to leave this village urgently so that I can find a better life for us. I'll come back for you when I settle down. Please take care of Tamuka, you hear me."

"Can't I go with you, brother?" Kumbirai bemoaned.

"No, you can't go with me now. Who will take care of our young brother hee? I'll come for you. Don't worry, I'll come back."

He took off very early the next morning before the village came alive and could see him. He didn't want to say bye to his mother due to the bitterness he felt towards her and for fear of alarming his uncle, he was leaving.

The money he had was only enough to take him as far as the Zimbabwean border and there he was marooned for weeks. Fadzai had neither passport nor papers allowing him to cross over into Zambia. For days he was doing some small anomalous jobs to earn him some money to have a meal. As they mingled with bus drivers at the bus station, he began to acquaint himself with them. He observed a man they called Mr. Zuze for some time before approaching him.

"Mr. Zuze, I notice you work on the Harare-Chirundu route. I can be of help loading and offloading your bus whenever it arrives, and cleaning it. You can give me a few dollars for my food sir," Fadzai spoke almost kneeling to him.

Mr. Tamuka Zuze was lean and tall. His complexion was that of a sunburnt darkness. It was evident from some areas of his skin which still exhibited his original tone, which was light.

"No, young man, don't kneel for me. I've a few men I work with, but I'll consider your request just for the sake of your respect," he said. "There're very few young men left who respect their elders. You're one such a rare one."

"Thank you, sir," Fadzai remarked.

"What else can you do apart from cleaning and offloading luggage? Do you know anything about repairing vehicles?"

"I've not done such works before, but I can assure you I'm quick in learning. You can train me for a month, and I'll be able to do the job very well."

"All right. I'll come back to you soon. I'll try to find something for you."

"Thank you, sir. I'll appreciate it."

A few weeks later, Fadzai saw Mr. Zuze's bus drive into the station and he ran towards it. Upon sighting him, Zuze asked Fadzai to come on board as it left the station for the garage.

"How are you my good friend?"

"I'm doing fine, sir."

"What have you been working on nowadays, any permanent jobs you're doing?"

"No sir. The usual odd jobs."

"Young man I'll give you a job and you'll be based at the garage. I need you to look after the vehicles parked there still under repairs and help the mechanics there."

"No problem, sir, I'll do my best."

"A lot of truckers come in the night to rest or have their trucks checked before proceeding on their journey. You need to ensure that they're attended to. That means working night shifts as well." Zuze detailed Fadzai.

"Sir, don't worry about me. I can basically do anything you ask me to do."

"I'll give you a good pay for your work."

"Thank you, sir."

After a fifty minutes drive, the bus came to a vast walled site with big buses parked inside, while most of the outside space was occupied by trucks of various sizes. The top of the wall fence was barbed wired for security and a camera mounted right at the gate. After being identified, the heavy gate swung open. They entered the premises that looked quite neat for a garage. At the entrance to the site, on the right stood a well-designed one storey building which housed several offices. There was a well-maintained lawn surrounding the building with flowers strategically planted, giving a superb look. On the left were open bays where buses that needed repairs parked to be worked on. At the far centre wall was a store building on which was written, 'Spares and Requisites'.

"That's it," Zuze said as he pointed to a small house on the left side of the store building in the corner. "That's your place there."

Fadzai was stunned as the house was neat, built out of concrete blocks and well painted. His expectation was that of sleeping in abandoned broken down vehicles. He was surprised to see the well-organised place.

"You can go and freshen up and then come and have something to eat. I'll be in one of the offices over there." He pointed to the single storey building.

Fadzai came to the door leading to the small house, clutched the handle, turned it and it opened into a living-room. He entered this well-furnished room with two settees placed neatly, making an L-shape in the medium-sized room. A black and white television set sat on a small coffee table near the centre wall. There was a small passageway leading to the bedroom, toilet and bathroom. Another door at the far end of the living room led to a small kitchen. In the kitchen stood a high stand and placed on it was a two-plate cooker and the other side was a sink. He gasped with amazement because to Fadzai, all these things were new as he led a typical village life before now. After having a shower, he joined Zuze in the office building, and they chatted with another man in charge of recruitment.

"Welcome Fadzai to Gritham Garage. I'm Mr. Ariko Banga. I believe Mr. Zuze has detailed you on your work."

"Yes, sir."

"You'll be given work schedules to enlighten you on your work for the day. Any questions?"

"No, sir."

"You can go with Mr. Zuze. He will orient you."

As they walked out of the building, Fadzai confided in Zuze.

"I've seen a cooker in the kitchen. I'm not familiar with how to use it. Kindly show me before you leave."

"No problem Fadzai. First, let's get something to eat by the general kitchen and then we deal with your kitchen later. I'm starving."

They entered the canteen and found a few of the workers about to finish eating their lunch. Two groups of about six or seven were seated in the hall and they instantly turned to see the new comers.

"Hallo, guys!" Zuze greeted them.

At that moment, a lady appeared through the swing doors of the kitchen and received their orders. They took the seats closer to the exit. After a few minutes, she swung the doors open again and called out Zuze's order. He approached the counter and came back with a tray packed with food. The smell of dried fish made Fadzai's stomach grumble. The last meal he had had was lunch the previous day.

Fadzai found the food delicious, a significant difference from the ones prepared at the bus station.

Later in the evening, after acquainting Fadzai in his new environment, they entered his cabin.

"My good friend you've got a pleasant house here, don't you?"

"Yes sir. It's all thanks to you."

"Never mind. You mentioned not knowing how to operate the cooker. Do you know how to switch on this television set?"

"No. I don't know Mr. Zuze. I don't know its use."

"Hahaha, my friend you haven't lived anywhere apart from the village hee."

"Yes sir. I was born and grew up in my home village."

Zuze pressed a small round button and light came to the screen. Slowly, some figures began to show and eventually it became clear. Fadzai was stunned at what he saw.

"How did these kids get in there?"

"Hum, don't worry my friend, you'll see more of them. You saw how I switched it on, didn't you?"

"Yes, I did. You touched at that small thing and this box came alive."

"Okay, my friend, you'll learn a lot of things. Let's go into the kitchen now."

Zuze led the way into the kitchen and gestured for Fadzai to move closer.

"This is a stove. It releases heat for you to cook your food in place of firewood at the village. Have you seen these numbers?"

"Yes, sir."

"I know at least you can count and have seen numbers before. Bring your hand here."

Zuze got hold of Fadzai's hand and together they screwed

the nob for switching on the cooker from zero to four, anti-clockwise, which screeched a bit.

"If you want to cook fast and need more heat, you increase on these numbers like this."

Zuze took the nob pointer to six, the maximum, as he demonstrated to Fadzai.

"Feel the heat coming up?"

"Ah, it's very hot!"

"Yes. You can now cook your food."

They went back into the sitting room. Fadzai was astonished and a surreal feeling still gripped him by the experience of this whole new environment.

"How did you end up in a beautiful place like this one, sir?"

"My father was good friends with a certain white man by the name of Mr. John Gritham. He owned this garage and asked my father to come and work for him. He took up the opportunity and left his master's farm where he previously worked, to go and work for Mr. Gritham. He was a very good man, and he treated us very well. When my father passed away, he asked that I replace him by offering me the bus that you see me drive. That's how I found myself here."

"Is he still around, Mr. Gritham? I haven't seen any white man around."

"Mr. John Gritham senior himself passed away three years ago, but his son now runs this garage. However, he's based in Harare and comes at least twice a week. He has entrusted this place to me and the manager whom you'll soon meet. That's why he took you in on my recommendation."

"Thank you, sir."

"Okay, I'll be on my way now."

"Thank you, sir, for everything. I don't know how to thank

you enough."

"Never mind. It's my pleasure to help you my good friend. Just don't let me down. I know you to be good and a hard worker."

"Don't worry about that, sir, I won't disappoint you."

The days started as usual with picking up the schedule for the day. Fadzai was now familiar with the routine work in the garage. About seven months had passed, and he fitted into the system very well. He was always ready to assist the mechanics and was himself becoming one. He could take up some of the easy jobs and repaired the vehicles also. In the night, he welcomed the truckers who were parking their trucks at the garage and made them comfortable. Those that needed repairs, he'd attend to the less complicated works while he left the more complicated ones to the trained mechanics.

Mr. Gritham junior was pleased with Fadzai's work and he from time to time borrowed him to work at his house. He'd go once or twice in a week to mow the lawn and plant and water the flowers at his house. This day he was busy working at the garage with one of the mechanics who went by the name of Akudwe Maphosa. They were bringing down the gear box of a bus. Fadzai was under the bus as the engine came down and landed on top of his left hand. He yelled in excruciating pain. Akudwe panicked. He called the manager who came and inspected Fadzai and rushed him to the hospital.

The phone rang several times before the voice of Gritham answered.

"Good afternoon, sir? This is Gamba. We've a problem at the garage." Garai Gamba was the garage manager. He was tall and dark with white eyes that popped from their sockets like those of a frog. The garage workers made fun of him, but he was a serious man who didn't mind there ridicules. He was very good friends with Zuze, and this made him like Fadzai as well. "I'm sorry, I've bad news, sir."

"What's the problem, Gamba?" Gritham spoke in a British intonation.

"Fadzai has had an accident, and he's at Harare General Hospital."

"What sort of accident?" Gritham asked impatiently.

"The engine fell on him as he and Akudwe worked on one of the customer's buses."

"How bad?"

"The x-ray reveals that his hand just above his wrist is broken and needs plates to fix."

"Oh no. Akudwe has always been in a hurry doing things. I've warned him before to take his time. See what he has done to his colleague. Do whatever you can. I'll come and settle the bills when I come there."

Fadzai spent one week in hospital, then was discharged. It was another month before he could start handling any work. Zuze dropped by to see how he was doing.

"My good friend, how are you now?"

"I'm feeling much better. I'll soon have this plaster removed then wait for the plates to be fixed."

"You'll be all right, Fadzai."

"Yes. I'll be all right; it's just I'm bored here with so little to do."

Late one evening, after Fadzai had put in a day's work, relaxed on his small single bed in his room. He'd had his hand operated on and plates screwed into his left ulna bone. He had recovered very well and he was now working quite normally. It was very hot that night and the air was dry. He was lying right under a wide-open window, his curtain blowing from the breeze that came in, but he could not find sleep. He reminisced about his home village and solemnness gripped him. He worried about how his brothers and mother were doing. He felt nostalgia. He thought of visiting them. To boast about his new life, his job, but his grandmother's words came back to him. How that he had to find his uncle in Zambia.

"I wonder why grandma sent me packing hurriedly like that. She mentioned of having a sickness that was incurable and how my father died. It's all very confusing. Can I go back so that she can explain to me or what?" Fadzai thought out loud to himself.

A knock came on his door that disturbed his line of thought. It was a customer coming to park his truck, and he quickly attended to him. Returning to his cabin, he turned on the television and was lost in watching a movie. He was feeling refreshed the following morning as he prepared to go to Gritham's house. As he entered the premises, Gritham was driving out.

"Hallo, Fadzai. How are you doing now?"

"I'm well, sir."

"So, are you well enough to come for work?"

"Yes sir. I can do some watering of the lawn and flowers."

"All right, if it's okay with you. I'll see you later. Have a lovely day."

"Thank you, boss."

They were seated at the small veranda of Fadzai's house. He and Zuze enjoyed a discussion when he decided to talk about something that had been on his mind and was unsettling him.

"Sir, I wanted to ask you for some help," he said.

"What is it that you want me to do for you, young man?" Zuze asked.

"I left my village to go and look for my uncle in Zambia. I know you've done a lot for me. Without you, I'd have found it hard to survive. But that's the reason for my coming here and I need to cross into Zambia. I need to fulfil my grandmother's request, but I don't have a passport to cross over. Please help me, I know you've connections," Fadzai pleaded.

For a moment, Zuze looked down and was staring at the ground in empty space. Fadzai searched his stare to decipher what Zuze was thinking to no avail. After some time, Zuze then lifted his head and spoke.

"I know it's important for you to do what your grandmother told you, but don't you think it's risky to enter into territories you don't know? Look for a relative you've not seen in a long time and have never visited before?"

"I know it's dangerous. One would have opted to stay here and continue working, but I need to do what I was told, to be at peace with myself."

"You've been a well-behaved young man. I like you and so does everyone here. If you left, I won't know whom to replace you with. You've done almost all works I've given you."

Zuze rubbed his small beard that had turned grey and was scattered on his chin, frowning at the unexpected request.

"All right, just give me some time and I'll work on your request." Zuze snuggled Fadzai by his shoulders. "In the meantime, continue with your everyday work. I'll be facilitating for that in the background." He assured him with a grieving countenance.

Chapter 3

Fadzai managed to cross into Zambia using a travelling document organised by Zuze, but was soon stuck at the border. The bus station was open, with no shelter for Fadzai to sleep in. It was busy with bus conductors and hawkers yelling to attract passengers and customers as they sold their food stuffs and fruits. The place was crowded with buses and tankers carrying fuels and trucks full of goods. He walked around in search of a place to sleep. Looked among the big trees around but none seemed to be ideal for his night crashes as they were in the open. He noticed a trench that was abandoned by motor vehicle repairers. These were not strange to him, as he saw many of them at the garage back at Gritham's. He looked for a zinc metal sheet and covered the upper side of the trench while the other side remained open. He'd sleep there for days, covering himself with boxes and sacks. He thought it was more habitable than the open space. The trench was also home to mosquitoes, cockroaches and other creeping animals. The weather at Chirundu was not so idyllic as it got extremely hot during summer. The area was circled with bush. Lions and other animals came around to eat food that was thrown all over by travellers. On many occasions, Fadzai heard lions roar and remained unmoving from fear to prevent them from eating him. International Police and Immigration officers made deliberate inspections on illegal dealings and immigrants. They demanded identification on the spot. Several arrests were made of individuals who didn't produce their identification cards and were deported back to their countries. Vehicles were searched thoroughly for any illegal items and smuggling of uncleared goods. This happened while Fadzai looked on as he himself was ignored due to his now tattered appearance and being a regular figure around the place. Several trucks parked waiting to be cleared of goods they were transporting. Truckers gathered in groups chatting, waiting for the clearance process that took several days. They spoke at the top of their voices about their trip experiences, what they saw along the way as they waited. Fadzai went closer to eavesdrop on their conversations. From his assessment, the groups that comprised of new faces daunted him to proceed with his plan to leave the border.

After staying at the border for about a month while in the cabin he made for himself, Fadzai's eyes lingered at its entrance. He was relaxing from the heat of the evening. From nowhere he saw a lion on the chase after an impala. They ran past the bush near the border at full speed. Billows of dust rose, but the lion was unsuccessful and went back into the bush. A few days later, Fadzai saw the same lion emerge from the bush to look for food. It looked sickly. It approached near to where Fadzai was staying and strode towards him seemingly in slow motion as if to lure its prey. It was in broad daylight and the lion focused on him. It was a rare occurrence to see lions come out during the day and loiter around the border. Fadzai was petrified, shaking like a leaf as lately, a lot of fleshless bodies were found with only heads, hands and legs still stuck to them. This was evidence of lions eating humans. The lion stooped and was directly at the opening of his makeshift cabin and looked straight at him. His mane was bushy and intimidating. He roared loudly, making everything near it to tremble. Fadzai was stiff and coiled himself with fear, his stomach rumbled, head between his huddled legs and hands clutched to his head, preparing for his death. His teeth chattering. Where he was seated, he just discovered his trousers becoming wet. Rising again, the lion strode even closer to him sluggishly. While this was happening, the people around watched in awe. When it reached the entrance of the cabin, it turned to put its back to Fadzai. After a few minutes seeing there was no action, Fadzai slowly lifted his head, noticed a big stick lodged in the lion's side that protruded, disturbing it. It seemed the lion had the stick stuck in its ribs for days and that caused the wound to start rotting and attracting flies. It sat as though waiting for Fadzai to do something. He gathered courage, went towards it, held the stick and with strength pulled it out. The lion roared, then jumped in pain and ran into the bush as Fadzai also fell in the other direction. He remained astonished at the mysterious way in which the lion behaved and that it didn't attack him. He stood up but his knees were jelly like, trembling vigorously. His hand could not hold on to the stick, which slipped off and fell to the ground. He was so traumatised. A small crowd of people came around who had witnessed the action, and couldn't believe Fadzai was still alive.

Days later, the same lion appeared with a kill and brought it to the entrance to Fadzai's habitation and left it there. Fadzai watched the bizarre behaviour, and after the lion walked away, he peered outside and, seeing that it was clear, got the meat. He roasted it and ate it. The lion did this very act every time it had a kill. It could come over sometimes and sleep near to Fadzai's dwelling. When the other lions come looking for a hunt and strayed closer to Fadzai's cave, the lion could fight them, preventing them from attacking Fadzai. He realised the lion was trying to save him from any harm around that place. It was protecting him even from other wild animals. He was no longer an alien or a threat to Fadzai's life. Fadzai named him *chengetai*, meaning *'to protect or take care of'*. He stayed there for two months while under the protection of chengetai. This was a mystery to him.

Early one morning, while the sun was brilliant, Fadzai roamed around the compounds of the border. Activity was at its peak, like every other day. Travellers running to queue up and have their passports cleared. Businessmen and women also queuing to submit their papers for clearance. This time around, he saw a group of men seated under a tree chatting among themselves and decided to ask for a ride from one of them; a face he was accustomed to and saw quite often crossing the border. He approached the man and made a modest appeal.

"Excuse me, sir, I'm trying to get to Lusaka, but I'm stuck here as my money has run out. Please assist me by transporting me in your truck."

The gruffy man was holding a stick in his hand and he sought to whip Fadzai. He bolted for safety.

"Get away you street kid! You're the ones that steal our goods when we pick you up," he scolded.

Fadzai ran very fast, scared for his life as he felt already exposed in that neighbourhood. He went back to the trench that had now become familiar and a place he called home. He remembered back home that even if they lived a difficult life, it was far better than the current situation in his life.

"Uncle is a very weird and vicious man. He treated me and my siblings very badly since the death of our father. He got everything we had, but he didn't deny us food. I had a place to lay my head to sleep at Grandma Tinashe's. It was not the best, but it was restful. Then I had a wonderful job at Gritham Garage. I wish I had listened to Zuze and stayed there, continued with my job." Fadzai muttered to himself.

"Is life this hard? Grandma Tinashe never prepared me for this. I should have remained in Zimbabwe, someplace there and lived my life. This is too difficult for me," he said as he sat huddled, knees in his hands and tears rolling down his cheeks, wetting his clothes. He said a prayer and fell asleep.

Fadzai was woken by noisy baboons scrambling for some oranges a traveller left on the dashboard of his car. His driver window was wound down and the apes vigorously attacked each other as they helped themselves. Fadzai quickly startled them by chasing after them. The owner of the car had gone to buy some food from one of the restaurants nearby and was now walking towards his car when he noticed what was happening. He stood some distance away from the scene, as he knew too well baboons attacked people who seemed to intimidate them. He was scared and equally worried that if a lot of them entered his car, they would tear away his seats and carry his luggage. The man looked on as Fadzai skilfully dealt with the baboons as though he was one of them. It was like they understood very well the language he spoke, and they followed wilfully. He was very pleased with Fadzai and he called after him. "Hey young man, come over here!" Fadzai rushed towards the man, bending down holding his knee as a show of respect, which was one of his virtues and he greeted him. "What's your name, young man?"

"I'm Fadzai," he responded quickly.

The man was of medium height, build and dark in complexion. He was casually dressed in black jean trousers and a white long sleeve t-shirt. He had a heavy accent in his speech of a typical African man that was attractive. His hair was well cut, giving him a very handsome look.

"How did you manage to send the baboons away without being attacked? You did it so well."

"I've come to know a few tricks on how to handle them, sir. I was just afraid they could have messed up your vehicle, sir."

"I'm very thankful. And how much do I owe you?"

"No sir, I did that to help, not to be paid."

"What, then can I possibly offer you for this act of bravery?"

"Sir, I'm trying to get to Lusaka to look for my uncle, but I've been stranded here for months without food and covering. Would you give me a ride if you're going in that direction?" The man was shocked and felt remorse for Fadzai that he was quick to mention…

"I'm passing through Lusaka on my way to Ndola and would appreciate some company and would definitely be glad to help out."

Fadzai was now looking very shabby with an overgrown afro. His beard was also overgrown, giving him an ugly and older look. The stranger paid for him to have a shave, a shower, and bought him new clothes and some food.

"Ha, I didn't know you were very handsome and light," the man complimented him after his shave. Fadzai thanked the man as he gave a sheepish smile.

"We should go to the port office to see whether the goods have been cleared so that we can start off today." Fadzai was known to the clearing officers around that place. He quickly talked to one of them and in an hour everything was ready.

"How did you do that?" The man was perplexed.

"What, sir?

"My papers didn't take long to be processed."

"Oh, I used some of my acquaintances to facilitate the process, sir."

"I didn't expect that efficacy," the man remarked.

They organised the goods and parked them into a light truck.

"Young man, put the rest of the bags into the trunk of the car."

Fadzai went around the car and put the bags into the boot. In no time they were on the road. He wound down the passenger window and allowed the cool breeze to hit his face. He could smell the moist soil, which was wetted by some rain showers and various sweet fragrances of wild flowers. In the car, the man asked how Fadzai, as young as he was, could take off on such a dangerous journey looking for a lost relative.

"It's like looking for lost treasure without a map," the man teased. "What really caused you to make such a decision coming from a far country entering into foreign land, and expecting your uncle to still be at the address you were given?"

Fadzai began to narrate how he had to run away from his own relatives because of succession matters.

"I took off because there was no one to hide me, so my grandmother thought it was a good idea to send me to die away from my people," tears were running down Fadzai's cheeks as he talked to the man.

"What do you mean hide you? Were the matters fatal?"

"I believe so, sir. My grandmother only told me to pack up and leave the village before I die mysteriously like my father. I didn't know why and what she meant. I was not to return to my village if she passed on. That's the information she gave me, and there was no time to find out more. It was an emergency of sorts."

"That sounds petrifying, but hey I guess your grandmother found herself between a rock and a hard place and had to do what she thought would be best. Man-up and do whatever is necessary to survive," the man lectured.

Fadzai felt challenged by the man's advice, which could be detected in his firm voice. He dabbed on his tears with his shirt and said, "I can manage to survive even if I don't find my uncle. I've worked before while I was in Zimbabwe and had been at the border for over three months. I learnt a few survival skills. I did small favours for the visitors at the border and they gave me a tip or food to eat," he said smugly.

"That's more like it my son. That's the spirit," the man flattered him.

"I discovered there're so many things travellers didn't know and when you step in and offer them your services, they'd pay you." Fadzai expressed his newly acquired knowledge with flamboyance.

"I hope you didn't involve yourself in illegal dealings. I know a lot of drug dealers using young vulnerable boys like you to transport their contrabands into and outside the country. Before you know it, you're caught up in a clutter of snags."

"No sir, I'm very careful what I engage myself in. I come from a poor background so I can't afford to entangle myself in such issues."

"Yeah, be very careful, son."

"Yes, sir."

The man cleared his throat and began, "I'm privileged to have grown up in a well-to-do family. However, this is not what defines my future. My father owns some businesses and sent me to good schools. I've studied outside the country and just finished my master's degree in economics in the UK. My passion is in business just like him, so this is what you see me do. I believe that I don't need to relax because my father is successful, no. I need to prepare for my own future. So, don't think I'm better off than you. What you need is to just believe that you can make it. Capital to start a business does not only come in money form and not only the learned make it in life."

"Yes sir," he spoke with elation. "I just need to work hard and discover my strength."

"That's the way to go, Fadzai."

As they drove on the Chirundu–Lusaka road, Fadzai was amazed by the natural wonders of Zambia. The mountainous terrain and a lot of bush reminded him of his home country.

"This is an amazing view. Zambia is a very beautiful country." Fadzai said.

"It's also full of wonderful people. Zambians generally are a peaceful and loving people. They're hardly violent and are very welcoming," the man said.

"Our country's land is largely used for agriculture. However, I've seen a lot of bare land here in Zambia, any reason why this is the case?" Fadzai inquired.

"My son, as you've seen, this area is mountainous, and not many people live around here." They got to a place where there was a stone pillar.

The driver explained, "When travellers come to this place, they paint on that stone there," pointing to it, "marking their passing by it. That's how it earned its name, Red Paint."

"It's an epic place."

"You can call it that if you want. Just like Doctor David Livingstone, wherever he passed, they erected pillars to mark his route like that one over there. Have you heard about him, I mean Dr. Livingstone?"

"No, sir."

He was Scottish and came as a medical missionary to Africa and reached Zambia. He discovered the Zambezi River and others. He rested in these places. When he died, his heart was actually buried under a baobab tree here in Zambia at a place called Ilala. Then his body was taken to Britain for burial.

They drove on into the mountains, and a hot breeze began filtering through the atmosphere as dusk approached. Fadzai wiped his head often.

"It is usually hot around this place as Chirundu is in a valley, laying along the Zambezi escarpment. That's why it's very hot in these expanses. When it's summer, from about August to somewhere in November, people usually sleep outside their houses, on their verandas, without covering because they can't stand the heat inside their homes," the man explained.

"I guess I experienced some of the heat when I was at the border. I didn't have proper covering, but I survived."

"Yes. You're lucky you stayed there around summer."

As they drove past some high hills, the driver said, "this place is called *four nyau*. You know what *nyau* means?"

"No."

"It's those clowns that dance at traditional ceremonies and wear masks with strange clothes sometimes made from animal skins or ripped materials."

"Ooh okay. I think we call them *zwinyawu* in our language."

"They were dancing at this same spot. A car came and hit them. They all died on the spot. That is why it's called *four nyau*, because four of them died at one go."

"That's sad."

"You'll also get to see when we reach a place called '*Kapili Ngozi Hills*' meaning Hills of Danger, where stones used to fall from the mountains like rain. They sometimes blocked the road and motorists needed to be careful when passing the same spot so as not to be buried by these rocks. A lot of accidents happened there. Some motorists, especially truckers, just failed to scale up the hills and end up veering off the road into the trenches as they lost control. The trenches are so deep, chances of getting out are next to none." The man spoke with regret in his croaky voice.

"Is there another route to use other than this seeming death trap of a road? The scenario you've just painted here is scary," Fadzai remarked.

"I didn't mean to scare you, son, but unfortunately it's the only major road connecting your country and others on the south to Zambia. The government is planning to repair the road as it's a very busy one and crucial for our trade in the Common Market for Eastern and Southern African region," he said.

"It's good that the government is looking into repairing this road," Fadzai said as the driver meandered the potholes on the road, slowing the vehicle down to about twenty kilometres per hour.

"Yes son, they just need to look at it seriously because truckers lose goods from thieves along this stretch as they move slowly, negotiating these potholes and ascending the hills. The thieves hide in the bush and when truckers come along, they climb onto the trucks and begin to off load goods. It has now become a norm that someone has to climb behind the truck to monitor these incidents, which is dangerous especially on the descent side. The trucks sometimes lose brakes."

They moved for a long distance while listening to some gospel music. They came to an area where they noticed a vehicle parked without seeing life around. The door was left open and the front windows were wound down. The driver moved slowly as he inspected the interior of the vehicle. There was no one inside it. He was curious and decided to stop and check around.

"I remember this man took off way ahead of us. Hours before we started our journey. He cannot possibly be here this time. The brother may have a problem with the car or something," he observed.

He got out of the car and went a distance into the bush after the man.

"Hallo, my friend! Hallo, someone!" he called out.

As he circled a big tree, he came running as though being chased by some wild animal. He opened the driver's door and got in the car with so much haste while pointing in the direction he came without speaking.

"What? What sir?" Fadzai asked as he also picked up on the man's fears.

"There! There!" he said as he banged his door and twisted the key to start the engine.

"What's there sir?" Fadzai continued to quiz the man in a panicky voice.

"A dead man. It's like his face had been peeled off," the man spoke in shock.

"Let's get out of here!"

He stepped on the accelerator pedal and sped off.

Tension was evident in the car as they drove for some distance without speaking a word to each other. Fadzai wondered what horror the driver saw that seemed to have visibly shocked him so much it registered on his face. His hands were still trembling, his face had turned grey and cold. They drove to a check point some kilometres from where they found the parked car. The man approached the police post and found two police officers.

"Good evening officers," the man greeted. "On my way here,

I saw a car parked with no one in sight and I checked if anyone was in trouble with their vehicle. When I inspected around, I saw a man lying dead behind a big tree with his face looking like it had been peeled off."

The police officer on duty whistled in surprise as he took down the statement.

"He must have parked in the game park. Stray Leopard most likely," he suggested. "You motorists ought to be very careful and observe the signs. You must not come out of your cars in the game park," he affirmed.

"Especially in the dark," the other officer standing in the doorway added. "We've had a number of cases of animals attacking motorists when they park to relieve themselves."

"We shall send a team to attend to the situation. Thank you for the information, sir."

"You're welcome and good day officers."

As the man was returning to his car, one of the traffic officers checking vehicles on the road pointed to his rear tyre.

"Looks like your tyre is punctured from a nail that is still wedged in it and is slowly losing pressure."

"Oh yes! I'll change it right away and have it mended when I get to Lusaka. Thank you for observing sir," he said.

They got busy changing the tyre. Fadzai pumped the jack and unscrewed the nuts, fitted the spare wheel and soon enough they were back on the road. Fadzai fell asleep while the driver drove on in silence. He had switched off his car radio as he felt it was making noise and caused him a headache. He covered a distance and, as he neared Lusaka, he woke Fadzai up.

"Where exactly are you going my son? We are almost reaching Lusaka."

Fadzai rubbed his sleepy eyes.

"What did you say, sir?"

"I wanted to know where you're going precisely?"

"I'm going to Lusaka International Airport, looking for Zambia Airways cargo office. I was told that's where my uncle works." Fadzai said.

"It's night now. Do you think you'll find your uncle there?" the man inquired.

Fadzai answered, "They work shifts. I'm hoping to find him or someone who can take me to where he lives."

A few hours later, they slowed down at the airport check point. The officers manning the check point inquired where the duo were headed.

"Good evening, sirs?" the officers greeted.

"Good evening, officers. We want to visit the Zambia Airways cargo offices. Where are they exactly?"

"You've just missed the entrance. Their gate is the one you've passed just by that building there," the officer pointed.

"Yeah right, it's actually printed in big orange and green letters there and we didn't see it. Thank you, officers."

"You're welcome, sir."

The gate was manned by a lean, tall dark man in uniform, holding an AK47 rifle. He waved to indicate stop, just as the car meant to enter through the gate. His face put on an irritable look that intimidated the two men.

"How can I help you?" he inquired.

"We are looking for Mr. Dulana Dube. We believe he works here," the driver spoke with his head poking outside the window.

"Why are you looking for him at this time of the night? How do I know you don't mean to attack him?" the guard spoke with sarcasm.

"Bookings are done during the day unless you book online.

I don't allow people after ten p.m. CAT unless at the passenger section or you're collecting cargo."

"Sorry officer, the young man needs some help to locate his uncle. He's coming from Zimbabwe and is not familiar with Zambia. I meant to help him before I part company with him," the driver said, now coming out of his vehicle. "Please sir, the young man needs your help."

The guard circled the vehicle and peeked through the passenger window to sight the boy. "What's your name, young man?" he inquired.

"I'm Fadzai Ncube," he replied.

"Come out of the car, I want to check you out," the guard said in a harsh voice.

Fadzai almost knocked himself down on the edge of the door as he came out, overcome with fear.

"Why are you looking for someone in the night?" he said.

Fadzai responded in a shaky voice, feeling more unnerved at the view of the man.

"I travelled the whole day with this man who assisted me. I've never come here before, and I didn't know we were going to reach here in the night."

Turning to the driver, he muttered "Mr. Dube works here all right, but he has knocked off. The next time we've a pool vehicle taking the few workers inside will be at three a.m. If you're lucky, they can take you to his home. In the meantime, you can wait in the guard house."

The driver clutched Fadzai's hands with both his hands while facing him and assured him, "You've found your uncle, you hear me. Don't worry, you'll be okay. I need to leave now. I still have a long way to go."

"Thank you very much, sir. I'll keep your advice in mind."

Fadzai said with tears lingering in his eyes.

"Young man, I wish you all the best that life can offer you."

Fadzai replied, "Thank you, sir. You've been kind to me."

The driver released the tight clutch on Fadzai and headed to his car.

Fadzai entered the guard house carefully and scanned the room for a place to sit. The guard pointed to a chair. "Take a seat. There's no fire or tea here to keep you warm."

"I'll manage, sir; I've passed through worse conditions compared to this one."

"What worse situations young man. What do you know about difficult times as young as you are?" the guard asked.

"I meant I've experienced scary and mysterious times on my way here."

As Fadzai explained, the guard's face took on a different countenance, that of surprise as he described his ordeals.

"Not even I, in my job have experienced what you've just explained here. It's quite frightening." The guard shuddered with fear. "It shall be well with you, son."

"Thank you, sir."

Fadzai made himself comfortable and fell asleep on the chair. He leaned on the wall his head slumped down. Moments later, the guard shook him with urgency and as he woke up, saliva ran down his mouth. As he stood up, he felt his neck stiffen from his earlier positioning. He stretched it a bit by pulling it on the back with his open palm, then stretched his hands above his head and let out a yawn.

"Get on your feet, son, pool vehicle will be out in a minute."

Fadzai organised himself, wiped the saliva on the side of his mouth as he followed the guard outside. A minibus slowed down at the gate with a high beam that blinded the view of Fadzai. He had to put his hand up to shield off the light as he stood in wait. The guard hurriedly approached the driver and conversed with him.

He then called out to Fadzai, "Son, hurry up and jump on board. They'll take you to your uncle's place."

Fadzai entered and made himself comfortable at the back of the minibus as it took off.

"Hallo, young man," the driver shouted to him as he viewed Fadzai in the rear-view mirror. "Do you have an idea where you're going?"

"No sir," Fadzai responded. "I've just come in from Zimbabwe and I've never been here before."

"Okay, I'll show you. No problem."

"Thank you, sir."

As the minibus sped, Fadzai watched the streetlights along airport road for the second time. From a distance, he saw airplanes as they took off and some landing at the runway of the Lusaka International Airport.

The minibus entered Great East Road past Chelstone suburb and made a left turn at Hybrid turnoff. He drove through National Resource Development Centre (NRDC) and came to a stop at a hedged blue house with rough casting at the bottom wall in the suburb of Mtendere. He sounded a horn and Mr. Dube came out of his four-roomed house, buttoning up his shirt he approached the driver.

"Is there an emergency?" Mr. Dube asked with surprise.

"Not at all, sir. I've brought a visitor of yours; I believe your nephew from Zimbabwe."

"My nephew?" He was curious.

"Yes sir, he's in the back seat," the driver turned to Fadzai.

"Young man, your uncle is here. Go out to meet him!" he

shouted.

Mr. Dube was shocked as he had no idea who the young man was now standing in front of him.

"Young man. Who are you?" he quizzed him.

"I'm Fadzai Ncube, the son of Runako and Maita Ncube."

"Oh my God! You're Runa's son?" Dube registered his amazement. "I didn't know he had a son at all. I haven't been to Zimbabwe in twenty-five years."

"Is everything okay, Mr. Dube? Can I take my leave?" the pool driver inquired.

"Oh yes, everything is okay, and thanks for bringing my visitor home. I'll see you later. C'mon in and tell me what brings you here."

Fadzai took the seat next to the door as Dube sat right opposite to him. "Tell me, son. How is everyone back home?"

"I left home over a year ago, but I believe they're all fine," Fadzai remarked.

"Where were you for that long time before coming here?"

"I was travelling and was stranded at some point in Zimbabwe. When I crossed into Zambia, my money had run out and I had to spend nights at the border. I could not find luck with help until a certain man offered to give me a free ride."

"Why didn't you announce your coming? I could have come to fetch you," Dube emphasised.

"My departure was not ordinary as Grandma Tinashe sent me on my journey with urgency," Fadzai said.

"Why is that?"

"Succession issues. She decided I leave immediately before something happened to me."

"You're talking about succession issues. Does it mean that Runako is gone?"

"Yes, sir. He died about two years ago."

"Oh, no!" He clasped his head in his hands and shuddered with grief. "I never received any telegram informing me about his death."

"Sorry for that, Uncle."

"I see. The kingship is in the lineage of your father's family. That explains it." Dube seemed annoyed. "So, who has taken the throne?"

"Itai, his stepbrother."

Dube paused for a while staring at the wall as though he could see through it, his left hand folded on his chest while his right hand was raised such that his fingers firmly clamped his chin. "So, they couldn't accept you being their king? They wanted it to themselves. But why did Grandma Tinashe send you packing?"

"She feared that my own family would bewitch me. She was not going to stand me dying at their hands. She preferred I die away from the clan. She then asked me to look for you."

"It's good you're safe now. Are you their only child?

"No. I've two brothers. Kumbirai who is thirteen years old, and Tamuka, seven years."

"Take your rest, then we can talk more at daybreak." Dube ushered him to the boys' room.

In the morning he introduced Fadzai to his family of four children. Fadzai further narrated how he moved from the village to Zambia. Mrs. Dube was quick to mention that even if the house was small, Fadzai was welcome to live with them.

Fadzai was raised together with his cousins and when he was thirty-two years, his uncle looked for a job for him as a porter with the airline. He was loved among the workers and the customers because of his humbleness. After working for three years, Fadzai's uncle counselled him.

"My son, you're now grown up and the space here has become too small. It would be better for you to look for your own place to stay and probably start a family."

"I'm grateful, Uncle for having welcomed me in your home. I've heard your advice. I'll move as soon as I find a place." Fadzai spoke appreciatively.

Chapter 4

He was blessed with a wife and seven children. Fadzai lived in a good suburb of Chelstone, where he raised his children. He lived a typical African life, with a lot of extended family members living in his home. Nieces and nephews, including orphans he adopted orphans name them, and his house was always full of people. Some would sleep in the living room and sometimes even in the kitchen. He retired and went to settle in Busoli land, Chongwe, which became their home village. Anashe was the fourth born of Fadzai. Anashe's mother passed away when he was in high school while two of his siblings were still very young. Fadzai had grown old that he could not manage to take care of the two young ones that were staying with him at the farm. When the others were in boarding schools, Anashe abandoned his education to help keep two of his youngest siblings. Life became unbearable that they could only afford two meals per day. Breakfast was tea made from burnt sugar, essentially taking in carbon with a cake made of maize meal. Warm water was mixed with maize meal and a bit of sugar to taste so that it could be made into a ball. It was then boiled in water to make a hard cake. Lunch was around four or five p.m. to cater for two meals, lunch and supper. They also survived on simple jobs Anashe took up. The money realised could barely meet their needs. Anashe then decided to look for a job in the city of Lusaka.

"Father, it has become difficult to make ends meet here in the village. I've decided to go and look for jobs that can pay reasonably well. I need your blessings to go."

Fadzai, with weeping eyes said, "My son, you remind me of myself when I was growing up. Misfortune came my way that was too big for me to handle. Your great grandmother had to send me away at a young age."

"You never told me, Father, and you don't talk about your family in Zimbabwe," Anashe protested.

"It has always been a hard thing for me to share. I left my siblings when they were young and have not been in contact with them. I recently got in touch with a cousin who knows where my immediate young brother is. I plan to go and look for them and reunite. Like I told you some years back, my mother, your grandmother, passed away, but I didn't attend the funeral. We can talk about that later, but today I'm also releasing you with the same blessing my grandmother, your great grandmother, released me with. God will be on your side. Go my son, go well."

Anashe arrived in Lusaka's Kaunda Square Stage 1 and looked for Mr. Ndhlovu who was coming from the same village as himself. He located him and lived with his family for a while.

One day, Mr. and Mrs. Ndhlovu sat down with Anashe and said, "Anashe, you need to find a place for yourself. We can no longer accommodate you here. We give you three days to look for accommodation."

"I haven't found a stable job yet and have nowhere to stay. Is it possible you give me at least a month?" he appealed.

"Unfortunately, we cannot extend to that long. Just prepare for your departure in three days."

Anashe was troubled by this development. He straight away looked for a place to live. In two days' time, he secured a one-roomed house in the same neighbourhood. He continued to do odd jobs that helped him pay for his rentals and food. He walked long distances of about five to seven kilometres every day, looking for jobs and the same distance back home. Life became equally difficult as when he was in the village, but going back was only going to worsen things. In his job hunts, he met someone by the name of Kondwani Sakala and they became acquaintances. Anashe could do some jobs with him while Kondwani could help Anashe in difficult situations. Kondwani was a transporter working with a public service passenger vehicle. He was a Christian congregating in a Pentecostal church, married but had no children. He invited Anashe to worship at his church occasionally and visited his home.

"I can see God has blessed you with a good wife. She has a good heart. I pray that God would bless me with a wife just like yours, Kondwani," Anashe said. She was Zimbabwean and Anashe quickly blended with her and called her his sister. It was like he had found family in Zambia.

"I thank God for her, but unfortunately we don't have children yet. We've been planning to have kids, but I believe God will bless us with the fruit of the womb," Kondwani said.

Kondwani's pastor called for prayer and fasting periodically. This one he called and encouraged the members at least to bring a friend who wanted God to intervene in their situation. When Kondwani saw how Anashe was struggling, he asked him to join in the prayer and fasting session.

"Anashe, you've been suffering for too long. Look, you're finding it difficult to get a permanent job for a while now. You can join us for prayer and fasting so that you can forward your petitions and allow God to intervene in your situation. I also want to petition God to heal and bless my wife with kids."

"I've never fasted in my life except in situations where I didn't have food. I don't know if I can manage," Anashe said.

"No Anashe, it's very manageable. Believe in God and in what you're doing, then everything will fall into place. I thought the same when I started, but now I'm used to it. It has benefited me a lot," Kondwani assured.

"It's true I've struggled for too long. It's time I allowed God to deal with my situation," Anashe spoke with a lot of conviction.

"Prepare around nine p.m. tonight to go to the mountain to return the following morning," Kondwani instructed.

"Believe me, I'll be ready at that time," Anashe responded.

At the agreed time, Kondwani entered Anashe's house as he readied himself for the night ahead of them. They carried a mat and some cardigans to keep themselves warm and left for the mountain. They reached the place of worship and found the pastor already there.

"You're welcome my sons. What do you want God to bless you with?" the pastor asked.

"Thank you, pastor. I've come with my friend. His name is Anashe. He has gone through a lot of hardships and requires prayers. He will explain to you himself," Kondwani retorted as he turned to look for a spot of his own to pray.

"My son take a seat and tell me what's bothering you," the pastor offered a stone to Anashe to make himself comfortable.

He explained to the pastor what he had been through in detail.

"All right my son, that is a lot of burdens but there's nothing that God can't fix. What, then are your specific prayer requests that you want God to deal with?"

"Pastor, I want God to give me a job and a good wife, just

like my friend Kondwani."

"Oh okay, as you've believed in God, also believe that your problems end here. You shall enter seven days of prayer and fasting, and God will answer you according to your faith," the pastor instructed. "Now go my son, and find yourself a place of prayer and converse with your God."

Kondwani and Anashe encouraged one another not to relent in their prayer programs and this helped Anashe to manage the fasting.

"I didn't think I'd handle it, but I feel even stronger and can pray for long hours," Anashe remarked.

"One only requires focus and determination, coupled with faith, that God will change their situation. I see you're very determined Anashe," Kondwani complimented.

"I want to be like you my friend. You've everything, a good wife, a job. That's what I want for myself."

"You'll have them and more. God is the giver of everything," Kondwani summed up.

Three days into their prayer and fasting, Anashe was asleep at home when Kondwani received a call from someone who was looking for a driver for a public service vehicle. That day Kondwani didn't see Anashe anywhere, so he checked for him at his house.

A knock came on Anashe's door.

"Come in please," he responded.

Kondwani entered the house.

"Ah, it's you Kondwa. What brings you here? Are you not working today?"

"You're here sleeping my friend; people are looking for you. There's a job for you to start working tomorrow morning. Let's go and you can meet the boss."

Anashe hurriedly picked some clothes to wear, prepared himself and the two were soon off.

"Good afternoon sir, Kondwani greeted the boss's son. This is Anashe, my good friend. The one I recommended for the job."

"Oh okay. Have you ever worked with public service vehicles, passenger transport in particular?" the boss' son inquired.

"Yes, sir. That has been my specialty for about a year now. No record of accidents, sir," Anashe answered.

"All right, I trust your friend Kondwani, as I've known him for many years. I believe he cannot recommend someone who can't deliver. You can start work tomorrow. The bus will be parking here, and you'll be picking it up every morning. Is that understood?"

"Yes, sir." A response came from Anashe swiftly.

"I believe Kondwani has filled you in on the conditions and by your coming to seek after the job means you're okay with them," the boss indicated.

"Yes sir. I'm comfortable with the conditions of service." Anashe gladly answered.

"I'll prepare a contract for you to sign," the boss said.

"Thank you then and see you tomorrow, sir."

There was jubilation after leaving Mr. Nkhosi's home and that evening Anashe was radiating with happiness as he was giving an account to the pastor at the mountain over the current development.

"Pastor, I've found a job as a driver and I'm reporting tomorrow," Anashe smiled.

"That's wonderful news my son. Only three days into your prayer and fasting, and God has already started answering your prayers."

"That's true, Pastor."

"However, he's in the process of granting your other requests. My advice to you is not to stop your prayer and fasting mid-way because God is answering your requests. Make sure you complete as instructed," the pastor advised.

"Noted, Pastor. I'll seek my usual spot for prayer now."

"Okay son. Will see you later," the pastor lay his hand on Anashe to bless him as he left.

Seven days prayer and fasting ended and life went on as usual. Anashe was working very well and things moved on just as well. He met Mr. Nkhosi himself. He was a tall well built handsome man in his late forties. He had a fair coloured complexion which caused Interpol to follow him, thinking he was a foreigner, particularly from South Africa. He was ngoni by tribe and his name was found mostly among the ngonis of South Africa.

"Ncube, the name is familiar. Which Ncube is this one? Is your father working?"

"No, he retired a good fifteen years ago."

"Where was he working?"

"He used to work for Zambia Airways cargo section as a porter."

"I know your father. I worked with another of your relatives, *eh...* a Mr. Dube who was his uncle. Do you know him?"

"Yes sir, when my father came to Zambia, he was the one who took him in. He lived with him for a while and he was the one who found him the same job, sir."

"So, you're no stranger to me at all. I was renting your

uncle's house in Mtendere where your father also lived. That's where I had four of my eight children."

"*Eeeh*," Anashe was bewildered.

"I came to Lusaka when I was quite young, about twenty years of age. I had just completed my senior secondary school in Chipata – Eastern Province and was picked to work for Zambia Airways. When I joined the company, I found your uncle working there. I was initially accommodated by the company and given time to look for my own accommodation. He got wind of the matter and offered me his house if I liked it. I took the offer and lived there for about five years. Your people are wonderful people. This gives me a lot of comfort seeing how good and hardworking your parents were." Mr. Nkhosi showered compliments.

"It's good to know that I'll not be working for total strangers, but family," Anashe concluded.

"It's a small world. Feel at home, young man, and greetings to your father when you go to see him."

"Yes, sir, I'll convey the greeting."

Chapter 5

As he worked for a good two years, Anashe became familiar with the boss's daughter, Tamara. She had just graduated from senior secondary education and was preparing to go to college or university. As a pastime she played basketball, tennis, volleyball and some soccer but her real passion was in volleyball. She played professional volleyball at club level with Barclays Bank and Bank of Zambia teams. Anashe and Tamara met once in a while on her way for training at the sports complex. Occasionally, she'd use her father's bus, which Anashe drove.

Tamara was on the bus that day and Anashe was on the phone talking about a church overnight program with Kondwani which got her interested as she was passionate about God.

"Where is this overnight prayer program taking place?" she inquired.

"At our church in N'gombe Township," Anashe responded.

"I'll attend one of your prayer sessions one of these days," she said. Tamara's family was from a Christian faith. Her parents belonged to a denomination of which Tamara didn't believe in. She didn't agree with the doctrines of that congregation that when reciting some of the prayers, she kept silence in disagreement of them. Her parents made it clear that as long as one lived in their house, they were to go to the same church. It was Tamara's prayer that after she found employment and left her parent's home, she'd look for a church where she could worship

God in truth and in Spirit according to the way she understood the word of God. She could not say she was living in truth as areas around her life still felt that she was in bondage. The preaching of that congregation was not engaging. Tamara thought that if God was a Spirit and omnipresent, then she could have a conversation with Him, and He'd hear her. She could speak to him every day about what she wanted to do and what God should do for her.

"I want you to show me a true servant of yours who can preach to me your truths. I don't feel I'm in the right congregation. If you do this for me, I'll do whatever you ask of me to do," she'd tell God.

"Good evening," Anashe greeted Semi the youngest son of Mr. Nkhosi.

"Good evening, Anashe," he replied.

"Here are the keys for the bus," he said and then added, "is your sister Tamara there?"

"Yes, she is," Semi answered.

"Kindly call her for me."

She was in the living room watching television and chatting away with her family. Unexpectedly, Semi whispered to her.

"Your friend is calling you."

"Who?" Tamara asked.

"The driver,"

She went outside after a while and pretended to be amused to see him. He asked about her every time he went to park the bus. The family came to accept that the driver was a friend of hers.

"Sorry for the slight delay. I was talking to my family otherwise I'd have come much earlier. How was work?"

"Work was okay. I just wanted to see you."

"Okay, that's kind of you."

"See me off to the station so I can catch a lift," he said in a jolly voice.

This went on for some time. He seemed to be very excited with their acquaintanceship that she noticed the habit of always wanting to see her, to be around her. This made her resolve to deliberately hide herself whenever he came. Tamara felt that by continuing to see him, she may lead him into thinking she could be more than a casual friend.

Zone six volleyball championship was on and Namibia was hosting. Rehearsals were on to select a team to represent Zambia. Bank of Zambia came out to be the team of choice to represent Zambia. In camp, excitement among players was at a hype. A friendly game was organised for team Bank of Zambia to establish preparedness and first best six and also which formation to use. Tamara was playing setter position. Mwitusha, one of the best spikers of the Bank of Zambia team, was playing on the opposite side to Tamara. The game was tough. Both teams put up their best. Tine was the best spiker on the side Tamara was playing. She was slender and tall. Mwitusha, though slender was slightly shorter than Tine. The ball didn't seem to hit the ground as both teams put up good defence at the back. As the game was in process, Mwitusha charged and hit the ball. They attacked on the net while on the opposite side the spikers charged together with Tamara to block the ball. Mwitusha missed the ball and only tapping it with her fingers, but the impact of her strike went full force on Tamara's fingers. Full pressure of her palm applied on Tamara's right ring finger. The third and fourth lumbricals of the hand tore as though it was fabric just at the point they connect to the palm so that the fingers hung loosely, dangling supported only by the skin that still connected to the hand. Tamara landed on the ground and held her fingers in pain.

"Ooh my finger!" she cried out.

Blood was oozing out of the cut, dripping on the volleyball court. The game came to an abrupt stop. The coach and the umpire checked on Tamara.

Immediately, Mwitusha trotted to the bench and dialled a number on her cell phone. She engaged in a conversation with the sponsor of the team.

"Hallo," Mr. Sakala.

"Hallo," he responded.

"This is Mwitusha, I've some bad news. Tamara has just had an accident. She needs to be taken to the hospital."

"What sort of accident?"

"I meant to spike the ball but missed it instead, it landed on her fingers. The ring finger slit and requires stitching."

"Ooh sorry." He agonised at the news. "I'm sending a driver right away to take her to Chainama hospital."

"All right, sir. He should hurry up because she's losing a lot of blood."

"Yes, my dear. Right away. He's coming right away."

The driver, Mwitusha and Tamara arrived at the hospital. As they entered the lobby, the doctor was there waiting and expecting them as Mr. Sakala had already communicated to him about their coming. Tamara was whisked away into one of the consultation rooms, blood trickling on the floor that trailed into the room. The doctor who went by the name James Ndhlovu examined the cut and recommended stitching right away. A medical trolley of instruments was wheeled closer to the doctor who put on gloves.

He asked the nurse to take her vitals and administer local anaesthesia to the hand to relieve the pain before stitching the lesion. Tamara saw the injection that was prepared and projected towards her hand that was in a lot of pain. She refrained the nurse by pushing her hand away.

"Mummy, we are trying to numb your wound so that you don't feel pain when the doctor is stitching it. Otherwise, if we leave it, it'll not heal properly and may cause you not to play volleyball again. Is that what you want?"

"No nurse. I want to continue playing, but there's too much pain on the sore and you want to prick on it with that needle, ha no!"

"It'll only hurt a little bit," Doctor Ndhlovu tried to assure Tamara.

Tamara looked away from the nurse and started speaking with Mwitusha. She squinted as the injection was entering her hand. The second one was not very painful as the anaesthesia had already started working. As the third jab was administered, she didn't feel a thing. Doctor Ndhlovu began stitching the finger. When he was through, he bandaged it.

"You shall be able to play full-time volleyball in two to three months. The wound should be completely healed by then."

"Thank you, doctor."

"You're welcome, my dear."

Before they left the consultation room and the grounds of the hospital, Mr. Sakala called.

"Are you done with Tamara?"

"I've stitched her hand. Though she will only play actively in three months, after the wound has fully healed. It was good there were no fractures or broken bones."

"Okay doctor, thank you."

That evening, as Anashe came to park the bus, he noticed that Tamara's hand was bandaged.

"What's the problem with your hand?" he inquired.

"I was playing volleyball and my teammate spiked my hand."

"What do you mean, spiked your hand?"

"In volleyball, when you hit the ball at the net with your palm so that you can score, we call it a spike. My friend Mwitusha, instead of hitting at the ball, she hit my fingers, and they tore. It happened so fast that before I realised, blood was all over the volleyball court."

"*Shi jeez!* What a tragedy. How bad?"

"One of my fingers was almost coming out. I had to go to the hospital without delay to have it stitched."

"Oh sorry! But you told me you were preparing to go for a tournament. Does it mean you won't go?"

"That's what it means, Anashe. I can't play for about three months, meaning I can't go."

"I'm so sorry to hear that. I know how you like the game and how you were looking forward to travelling."

"It's okay. I'll go next time. I guess it was not my time."

"Yeah." Anashe was remorseful.

That day was a Wednesday and the next training day was scheduled for Friday. Tamara went to watch her colleagues train. At this time, it had become known that she was not one of those travelling to Namibia. She was so unhappy as it was going to be the first time she'd travelled outside the country as an adult. She sat in the terraces watching her teammates train, quiet and miserable. Only a week had remained for the team to travel. The team sponsor, Mr. Sakala, came and was encouraging the team to get prepared for the trip. He turned to the terraces and saw a dejected Tamara who he treated like his own daughter. He had even employed her at his company as an accountant. Her colleagues thought she was his biological daughter. He called out for her to join the planning meeting for the trip just after the training. They discussed the readiness of the team with the coach and how they had suffered a setback with the dependable setter, in Tamara, due to her injury.

"Never mind, don't give up. The team will manage with the help of the second choice and if possible, when rotating, others can help in setting the ball as well," Mr. Sakala said. "As for you, Tamara, you'll accompany the team as one of the officials."

"*Eh*?" Tamara held her mouth in astonishment as the team roused in jubilation at the news, shouting their slogan, "Viva Bank of Zambia!"

The bus was made ready at around four p.m. and the team started off. They had delayed and needed to catch up on time, so they had no choice but to start off late. They passed through Munali Hills as the sun was setting. The bus laboured to scale up the steep hill as it was full to capacity with luggage packed on the back seat. The team reached Livingstone around ten p.m. Activity in Livingstone, a border town, was usually at a peak about this time and into the early morning hours. Prostitutes and hawkers were busy selling their merchandise. Night clubs packed with clubbers and drunkards. The team was stranded as they could not cross the border at that time of the night and didn't have money to book themselves into a hotel or lodge. The pontoon was open only from six a.m. to six p.m. The bus parked in town and the team gave each other turns to sleep in it. The group that was awake would entertain themselves by watching what was happening in the night clubs. Then the other group would go to sleep after some hours.

The team was at Kazungula border before sun rise and the office was not yet open. Soon the border was open and their passports were checked and in no time they were on the pontoon crossing. It was the first time Tamara was crossing a body of water and it was scary for her. She was made at ease as the journey on the pontoon would only last five to ten minutes. They entered Namibia's Caprivi Strip and continued with the journey. As they cruised through, they enjoyed a wonderful view of elephants as they are rampant in that area. They travelled about 500 kilometres and the team asked to park and stretch their legs outside and visit the bush to ease themselves.

After twenty minutes, the journey continued. It was becoming very hot as the bus passed through the desert area. The windows were all open but the air inside was as hot as the air outside. Several of the bus occupants picked up a book, a magazine or newspaper, whatever they could lay their hands on and began to fan themselves. They could not sustain the fanning as the air that was hitting their faces was still hot. They one by one began to drop their fans. After moving for some distance, some team members in whispers began to complain of a bad smell in the bus. When it continued, one player from the men's team, Choolwe, stood up and protested to his fellow players.

"Is it just me or are you smelling something bad in here? Driver! We need to stop and search the bus. Someone has defecated in the bus."

Laughter reverberated in the bus.

"It's not a joke. I'm serious."

They then sniffed the air in big snorts, as passengers one by one agreed with him. The driver pulled over and they began to disembark one after the other while the captain of the men's team checked the men and the female captain, the female players on their buttocks. When they were all out of the bus, they could not find a thing. Coming back on the bus, they checked the back of the shoes to see if anyone had stepped on faeces. For sure, it was discovered that one of the players had stepped on the stuff. They made him clean his shoes before entering the bus, settled in and the bus began to move again. Before long, the coach's phone went. It was the coordinator of the championship on the line. After their conversation, the coach stood up and addressed the bus.

"Listen up all of you. I know you're tired, and your legs are sore and numb from the journey. However, you're being awaited to play the home team Namibia University upon your arrival."

"*Uuumm.*" Murmurings flooded the bus.

"Calm down, calm down, I know it may be a gimmick to make us lose, but we will win. I'm counting on you, team. We will definitely win."

The bus was suddenly quiet the last hundred kilometres that remained to reach the University of Namibia. They were received very well and, just after putting their bags in the rooms that were reserved for them, they were on the court warming up.

The game was a tough one, but the team put in their all. The defence was porous at the start. Balls were falling at the base, making Namibia University gain leverage and points. The coach, Thawewe, was panicking and paced about in anguish. He shouted more often to the players to cover the back and the spikers to block on the net. On the bench, Tamara was filled with anxiety as she continuously jerked her legs in a rhythm that made a noise against the loose bench.

"Coach, I'm good at the back and I can help out."

"How can you even suggest that when you know your wound is barely a week from stitching? You want me to be fired by Mr. Sakala, your father?"

"No coach. He will not know as long as we don't tell him. See our team is losing, they're tired."

"There's nothing I can do."

"No coach, there's something you can do. You alone can allow me to play."

"Are you sure?"

"Yes."

"If you don't play well, you're out instantly."

"Yes, coach."

"All right, come."

Thawewe rose and approached the referee for a substitute. He beckoned to Tamara and as she walked towards him, he lifted his hand and curled it round her neck in a snuggle and brought her to the court line. The game was stopped by the umpire to allow the players to exchange. He signalled for a substitute to Pezo wearing jersey number seven. The team looked puzzled as Tamara, in jersey number three made her way onto the court. They gasped in shock but soon the umpire signalled for the game to continue. Back at the bench, Pezo who was substituted off the game, questioned the coach in anger.

"Why did you bring me out for Tamara who is not fit to play?"

"I'm the coach; I know what's best, so don't question me. Rest a while, then you'll go in."

The game was now fast-paced with defence solid. Tamara defended extremely well despite her wound. She didn't mention her wound had become painful due to the vibration of the ball hitting on the hands. It began to open slowly on the pressure of the digs of the ball that she restricted herself to and slowly began to bleed. Pezo asked if she could be put back in, but the coach said Tamara was doing fine. Tamara persisted until the end of the game. The umpire blew the last whistle as the ball touched down from a spike from Mwitusha that fell right behind the spikers in the zone area, earning the team three points and Bank of Zambia won the game. There was elation by the players, who lifted Tamara for having sacrificed and make them recover on the defence.

"Viva Thawewe! Viva BOZ!" they shouted.

The men's team was prepared. In the tournament, they clashed with Zimbabwean, Batswana, Namibian, Lesotho and South African teams. The Zambian team comprised of medium height players compared to giant, well-built tall players from the rest of the countries. They appeared to be the underdogs of the tournament. They managed to scoop fourth position with Zimbabwe coming in the first position, followed by South Africa then Botswana. The Zambian ladies team came in the second position with silver medals. They found Mr. Sakala waiting for them at the Bank of Zambia Sports Complex upon their arrival in Zambia. He didn't express much anger at the team's performances, as it was their first international exposure. He gave out allowances to each player as motivation and paid the officials.

"Tamara, I appreciate your sacrifice for the team. I know you played even when you had an injury."

"How did you know, sir?" she asked.

"Just know that the information got to me. It was a wise decision, coach."

"Thank you, sir."

Tamara looked at the coach and smiled heartily.

When Tamara told of her experience to Anashe, he became interested in the game and followed up on how the game was played. He committed to find time to watch some games played at the complex. This improved their relationship.

Chapter 6

Anashe picked up Tamara and drove southwards toward Kafue town. They passed through Chilanga and came to a lodge that had just been opened in that area. It was a very lovely place. The lawn was well trimmed and the chalets very attractive. Anashe led Tamara to the garden where there were garden benches and umbrella trees which offered a wonderful shade. They were beautifully green and planted in line, giving them an artificial look. They sat and entered into an intense conversation. Tamara was startled as a group of workers came right behind her and broke into song to wish her happy birthday. She stood up and held her chest right where her heart is and was overwhelmed.

"Thank you very much," she said as the lady carrying the cake carefully placed it on the table and they left.

"Thank you, Anashe. Who told you of my birthday, because I didn't?"

"I asked and was told."

"I even forgot as no one wished me a happy birthday this morning. Thank you for the gesture."

Tamara looked through the small opening between her bedroom curtains as the moon let its light into the room. She meditated on the day's events. She pulled a pillow and hugged it tight and fell asleep. The night was clear and silent. In her dream, she was at the coast overlooking the sea. There was a ship on the open sea and suddenly it caught fire. Screams were heard coming from the ship. The people on board wanted to come out of the ship, but the fire was so strong that it consumed them. Spillage of fuel from the ship on the surface of the water caused the sea to light up in flames. The horizon looked a deep red, and the heat was intense. It was difficult to have a good look, but two survivors were seen from a distance shouting for help. They clambered up the bridge ladder onto the bridge. Holding on to the handrail, they waved for help to a helicopter that was seen hovering over the ship's wreckage. The helicopter lowered a rope ladder and one of the rescuers waved to the survivors to hang on to it. They quickly held on tight, and the helicopter began to move, swinging them over the sea. They began scaling the ladder as the helicopter moved. It disappeared and immediately Tamara ran towards the guard house along the shore.

"Excuse me, sir, where is that helicopter going to?" she yelled while pointing in the direction it went.

"To the train station, mum. Not very far from here! Follow the coast to the north, you'll find a small town just there. You can't miss it mum!" the guard instructed while busy fiddling with gadgets calling for help. She began to run and could hear him calling into his phone "*Mayday, mayday*" then fading as the distance grew between them.

She ran for the train station. On her way, she met Kondwani and his wife who seemed surprised at the panic that reflected on Tamara's face.

"Tamara, why do you appear muddled and so in a hurry?" Kondwani inquired.

"Your friend Anashe was on a ship and it was destroyed by a fire. The two survivors have been taken to a train station not far from here. I need to go and check if he could be one of the two."

"Is that so?" Kondwani's wife retorted.

"I'll need your help to put up a façade, as no one can enter a transit point. It's only for the travellers already on the train," Tamara said.

"What can we do?" Kondwani was concerned.

"Good evening, sir," Kondwani tried to engage the guard in some conversation to distract his attention away from the entrance, so that Tamara could make her entry into the station.

"I meant to ask where I can buy train tickets?" Kondwani said.

As the guard was attending to the couple, Tamara entered the building and looked around, but could not see Anashe. She then focused on a figure at the counter in a coat and cargo pants. She walked towards him and called out, "Anashe?"

He turned to face her, and seeing that it was him, Tamara began to admonish him.

"I thought you were dead, but you're here sipping some juice. Don't you know I was scared, and you don't seem bothered by this at all?" Tamara continued.

Anashe just smiled and didn't respond to her. As she continued to speak at the top of her voice, Anashe spoke…

"Let's go and talk outside. We are attracting unnecessary attention here."

They went outside and Tamara picked up from where she left off while Anashe didn't speak a word. He stopped to stare at her and continued with his warm smile. As that went on, Tamara jerked out of her dream…

She was all sweaty and felt the fear grip her deeply. Her heart raced and she felt as though the dream was real. That was around four a.m. and she could not find sleep any more. She was bothered as it was a tendency of hers to have dreams come true. She thought this was one of them.

Could this dream be a vision? Could Anashe have survived this? What a mystery. She sought answers to her questions.

"What if he didn't make it as the dream depicts?"

Fear gripped Tamara, and she became restless.

"Anashe picks up the bus around five a.m.; I'll stay awake and make sure I'm the one to give him the keys." She was freaking out.

She waited impatiently until she heard a knock on the door. She jumped out of bed and quickly attended to the individual at the door.

"Good morning, Anashe?" Tamara greeted.

"Good morning," Anashe resounded.

"How are you today?" Tamara was eager to find out.

"I'm very well thank you. And yourself?"

"Very fine actually," as Tamara echoed, sounding relieved that what she had just had was no more than a bad dream.

Tamara went back inside the house to collect the keys from her mother. When she came back, Anashe was not at the front porch. She made her way to the back yard where Anashe used to park the bus. She found the doors wide open and the engine compartment open, but Anashe was not there. She went back to the front yard and, as she sought to go to the other side of the yard to check on him, she heard noises behind a hedge of flowers. She approached to inspect what it was all about and found Anashe vomiting violently. He had already vomited so much that he was very weak and barely standing up.

"Anashe, what's the matter?" Tamara questioned, her face clouding with worry.

"I don't know. From nowhere I just feel sick,"

"I'll be coming," Tamara spoke in a rush as she darted back into the house to call for help. She came out with her mother, who studied the situation. She then told Tamara to call Tandeo, her elder brother. Upon his arrival, they concluded that Anashe needed urgent medical attention and was to be rushed to the hospital as at this time he lay without speaking.

At Levy Mwanawasa Hospital, Anashe was examined and drips of saline water administered to him as he was dehydrated.

"What has he eaten this morning? Looks like food poisoning," the doctor suspected.

"I don't know what he may have eaten. He works for my father and he had only just come to collect the bus to go to work, but suddenly fell sick," Tandeo advised.

"He's in a bad state all right, but I'll try to resuscitate him and observe his condition. For now, buy fluids for him to take when he wakes up as we wait for the test results," the doctor further added as he left Anashe's bed.

Back at the Nkhosi's residence, Tamara panicked as the dream seemed more and more real. She could not understand how Anashe got sick soon after sighting her. It was like the dream was activated by their coming into contact. As soon as Tandeo came back, she sought to get an update on Anashe's condition.

"He's not doing too well, but the doctor is doing his best to revive him. He suggested food poisoning but could not tell what exactly until after the test results," Tandeo said.

"I need to get in touch with his relatives immediately. There's no one at the bedside."

Tamara was more frantic as she thought that Anashe was dying.

"I believe Anashe didn't survive as the dream foretold and that was why he was not speaking much," she spoke to herself.

How can I keep myself updated with his condition? I don't know any of his relatives, she thought.

Three days passed with no update.

"If Anashe was dead, we should have received the news by now," Tamara spoke as she paced around her room.

"I'll need to find a way to get the information." Tamara called her young brother. "Semi! Have you heard any news from the hospital about Anashe?"

"No, sister."

"Do you know where he lives?" Tamara asked.

"I went there once. We used the main road that goes to Kaunda Square Stage 1, then turned into a side road on the left and then... Ah! I think I can't remember very well how we moved and the particular house."

Tamara was very disappointed as she thought she was making progress.

"It's all right, Semi. I'm sure there're a lot of small paths and the place was new to you. I don't expect you to remember. Thank you anyway," Tamara assured.

She felt helpless as she waited for any news from someone. After five days, a boy Anashe worked with as a bus conductor showed up at the Nkhosi's residence.

"Good afternoon, madam," he greeted Mrs. Nkhosi, as Tamara looked on attentively.

"I came to report on Anashe's condition. He's out of hospital but still too weak to work. He will report as soon as he regains strength," he said.

"Thank you for the massage. I'll inform Mr. Nkhosi," Mrs. Nkhosi said. "Tell him to only come when he's fully recovered."

Tamara was hearing everything as she busied herself with tending to flowers, not to appear concerned. She was relieved to hear Anashe had been discharged from hospital. As the boy with the news was leaving the premises, Tamara caught up with him to inquire further.

"Hey, wait up," she waved at him.

"I overheard your conversation with my mother; you said Anashe is out of hospital?"

"Yes, madam. He's at home now but is not fully recovered," he reported.

"This means he's out of danger?" Tamara probed further.

"Yes, he just needs strength."

"Make sure you keep us informed every day about his condition; you hear me? You can call on this number." Tamara got a pen from her pocket and scribbled on a small piece of paper she picked up by the roadside and handed it to the boy, who sought to take his leave.

"Okay, thank you for the information and good day," Tamara announced as she turned to enter back by the gate.

A week later, Anashe showed up at the Nkhosi's residence looking skinny and out of balance from the illness. When he approached, he quickly asked for a seat as he was running out of breath from walking the short distance from the bus station.

"May I please have a glass of water?" Anashe asked.

"Okay, I'm fine, as I've noticed your urgency to have water." Tamara spoke as she entered the house to get him some water.

"How are you feeling now?"

"Better enough to even come this far," he answered. As he gulped on the water his Adam's apple yo-yoing as it pushed the water down his throat into his belly.

"I couldn't move. Now I'm walking. It's by the Grace of God that I'm even alive."

"We thank God," Tamara remarked, trying not to remember her dreadful dream.

"Is your mother at home? I presume your father is at work?" Anashe inquired.

"No, she has gone into town."

"I just passed to let them know that in three days' time, if I feel all right, I'll report for work," Anashe assured and took his leave.

Tamara remained asking herself what the dream meant.

"I dream that something happened to him and it immediately did. God, what are you trying to communicate to me? Do you mean that I should inquire about Anashe's life? Maybe you want me to help him with something?" Tamara audibly conversed with God.

Chapter 7

Anashe knocked off early from his job and seemed to have time to chat with Tamara. She was going to visit her sister and he offered to accompany her. When they came back from the visit, Tamara saw this as an opportunity and asked Anashe…

"Where do you stay exactly in Kaunda Square? I want to visit your home so that I can come to see you in case of anything. Like what happened when you were ill, I could not visit for that same reason," Tamara alleged.

Anashe sneered and then said, "My house is not in order and so you can't come!"

"I'm not interested about how your house looks like, but just to know where you live," Tamara insisted.

"Okay, okay, you win. Let's go, but I warn you, don't expect much."

Tamara and Anashe got on a bus to Kaunda Square. When they got to the community, she quickly noticed it was a massed house neighbourhood with uncoordinated pathways. She mused that could have been the reason why Semi could not remember the place. Then quickly she dismissed the thought. They reached Anashe's abode, and he invited her in. It was a one roomed unplastered house. The room didn't have a lot of things save for the bed in one corner and a two-plate cooker in another, with some pots and plates piled together in what appeared to be a cooking place. A string ran from one side of the room to another that served as an open wardrobe with some clothes hanging from it and an empty carton box for a washing basket. In a nutshell, tears were almost falling down Tamara's cheeks at the sight of this room which was full of potholes leaving a few patches of what once was concrete floor exposing soil in the house.

"I now understand the reason why God gave me the dream, so that I can help the brother," Tamara thought to herself.

She quickly started tidying up the place, not showing any emotions that would give her away, showing she felt sorry for him. She finished cleaning the house and soon they were busy chatting like old times.

"How has your life been before now?" Tamara asked.

"My life and my family's has been a difficult one. I came here to earn a living," he said.

Tamara listened ardently as Anashe explained.

"My father and brothers all depend on me for support," he added. "This is why I need to work extra hard to manage all their needs."

"Even if I may not have experienced your situation, I understand your burden." Tamara assured.

She immediately sought to take her leave, and Anashe accompanied her back to her house. She was troubled as she kept asking what God wanted her to do for Anashe.

"I know God wanted me to see his place and hear his story. Then what?" she quizzed herself.

"God, you always speak to me. I know you've spoken, but I've not gotten what you're saying clearly. May you give me an interpretation of this puzzle. Please my God…" Tamara prayed.

Early the next morning, Tamara went shopping in town. She bought some pots, plates, a washing basket and other household goods. She phoned Anashe who met up with her and she handed them over.

"Thank you very much, Tamara. I know you noticed a lot of gaps in my house. However, I'm thankful for the gesture," he smiled.

Tamara made another visit to Anashe's house. She questioned Anashe on how he managed his finances.

"I believe you generate quite some money from the job that you do. How do you keep it? How do you use it? Do you invest it or save in a bank account?" Tamara inquired.

"I use as I earn and keep the remaining money in the house. I don't earn much to have a bank account," Anashe responded.

"No, you at least make about fifty or hundred Zambian Kwacha extra money at the end of the day. Is that so? If you open an account and save that one hundred kwacha every day, you'll have three thousand kwacha at the end of the month and this is not small money you know," Tamara lectured.

"You're very right. If I save in a bank, I'll have a lump sum at the end of the month rather than keeping it under my bed inside the house; I'm tempted to use it. You make it appear very simple, yet making a lot of sense," Anashe was excited.

"I promise to open an account this week and save every excess money I make." Anashe assured.

He made savings every day, and when he came to check how much he had accumulated, he had more than what Tamara had estimated. This made him so excited.

"Anashe, where I work, we hire out vehicles and sometimes all our fleet is hired while our clients still need more. If you can find vehicles, we can sub hire from you and only get a commission. I'm sure the owners of those vehicles will give you a commission and you can make more money that way," Tamara advised.

"That sounds like a brilliant idea. I'll definitely put your advice to use."

He did as advised and made more extra money that he was able to start some small businesses. This improved his life and that of his family.

"God, I've done my part in the life of Anashe as you expected of me. I believe this is the time to let him stand on his own. Thank you, that you've answered his prayers," she said audibly to God, as was her habit.

Tamara went on with her life and only met Anashe occasionally, when there was some business to do together. Anashe seemed to do well as he was gifted with wisdom from God and blessings from the man of God that anything he laid his hands on worked. Still, Anashe felt this emptiness of missing something in his life.

"Ever since I stopped interacting with Tamara, it's not been the same. I'm doing fine, but something is missing," he spoke to himself.

I need to persuade Tamara to do business with me. As days passed, Anashe approached Tamara with a business proposition.

"Tamara, I've seen a broken-down minibus which we can work on and run as a public service vehicle and share the proceeds," Anashe suggested.

"That sounds good. We can buy and repair it. You're acquainted with the operations of public transport and you can easily run the business," Tamara said.

Plans went well and soon they were co-owners of a minibus. But little did they know they were slowly investing in each other's life.

"Tamara, I've been with you most of my life since I came

from the village. You've helped me from rags to the level I am now, where I can afford necessities and support my siblings," Anashe grumbled sorrowfully.

"That's very good Anashe. I don't know why you look sorrowful suddenly. I thought your progress was a good thing," she remarked, surprised.

"I've interacted with people who have come and gone and not affected my life. But you, I can't erase you from my life because you've made me what I've become. You hold a very special place in my heart," Anashe said.

"It's all thanks to God. It's His doing, not mine. I was just a vessel he used," Tamara smiled contently.

"No, what I'm trying to say is… Tamara I love you. I want you to be my fiancée," Anashe poured out his heart.

Tamara's eyes popped out in astonishment. She stood expressionless for a while, gazing into his eyes blankly.

"What do you mean, Anashe? You're my good friend. What are you saying?"

"What I've just said is that I love you and one day I want you to be my wife. Take your time to think about it. I know it has come as a shock."

Alone in her room, Tamara pondered on the proposal from Anashe. There's something special about this man. He has challenged me the way he has led his life. His selfless sacrifice for others and then… the dream? Was it a way of God bringing us together or what? What are my parents going to say? You want to get married to your father's worker? All these questions ran through Tamara's mind. From that time, the more Tamara wanted to hide away from Anashe, the more she missed his presence.

"You've been hiding from me for too long, Tamara. It didn't

mean when I proposed to you, you become my enemy," Anashe spoke from behind Tamara as she was watering the flowers outside the house.

She turned, startled by his voice.

"Oh, it's not that Anashe. It's that I've been thinking about what you said. You're late today. What happened?"

"I was held up by someone, but that's not important. Uhu, what have you decided?"

"I'm afraid of what my parents will think. What am I going to tell them, Anashe?"

"First of all, tell me what your thoughts are, Tamara? Is it a Yes or a No?"

"Uhuu… aah." Tamara hesitated while looking down.

Anashe extended his hands to cuddle Tamara's soft hands.

"Yes. What do you say…" Anashe spoke in anticipation.

"Yes. Let's give it a try."

"Wow! Thank you, thank you. Oh God thank you." Anashe kissed Tamara's hands with excitement.

"Let's deal with those questions about your parents later. We'll cross that bridge when we get there," Anashe said.

He entered into song, whistling all the way as he was getting the keys for the minibus to start his working day. In time, their relationship blossomed with a lot of love and wisdom. They worked even harder together than before. After one and a half years, Anashe and Tamara decided to make their intention to get married known to their families. Anashe approached a family friend of the Nkhosi's, Tamara's grandfather, and explained his intentions. The grandfather then spoke to Mr. Nkhosi who asked that Anashe come with his family and proceed with the marriage preparations.

Months later, Anashe came to collect the vehicle early morning around five a.m. as usual. He and Tamara had a little tête-à-tête.

"We are preparing for my cousin's marriage. My elder brother who is supposed to come and speak with your people is a little tied up. It'll take at least two weeks for him to set a day for a meeting." Anashe detailed Tamara.

"It's no problem at all. It's not like we are marrying just after the talks. It'll be sometime after the discussions so that we prepare our wedding. Don't worry yourself."

"That's good then. I'll see you later."

As soon as he left, Tamara and her sisters busied themselves cleaning the yard. She came across this strange concoction at the gate area and desperately dashed back to the house.

"Mother, come and see what's spread about at the gate."

"What is it my daughter?"

"I don't know. Looks like charms in a container and its content spilled at the gate?"

Mrs. Nkhosi went to inspect the odd stuff Tamara was talking about.

"Oh, this is not good. These were put here for someone to be bewitched. Did you touch this container or cross over the contents?"

"No, Mother. I only opened the gate and saw them."

"Touch nothing and don't go out of this gate."

Mrs. Nkhosi sent for Tamara's grandfather who came in a hurry. Semi fetched him and ushered him through the back entry at a small gate which opened to a small alley.

"Daughter, you sent for me. What's the matter?"

"There're charm like paraphernalia at the main gate. It's not known who put them there and why?"

"I see. I was surprised when Semi led me through to the

small alley when it's a longer route."

"Yes. I told all of them not to enter by the main gate."

"Oh, that's okay, but if someone has already gone past them, it has already used up its power and can't affect another person. That's how these things work."

"I sent for you so that you can help remove them. What are we to do?"

"I'll remove them don't worry. I'll burn them from the alley behind. Just take note of everyone who may have had access to this house. See if anyone gets affected by this and let me know immediately," he insisted.

"I'll be on a look out for that," she said.

"It's important because if not handled very well, someone in the worst-case scenario can lose their life."

"It's understood, Father. I'll do as you've advised."

A few days later, Anashe was hit with a severe back ache and he couldn't walk. He had a terrible fever. Severe weight loss was noticed in only a few days. Tamara visited him every day, but his condition kept deteriorating. Then she remembered the issue about the charm like substances at the gate. She recalled that day Anashe was the first one to enter by the gate and they had a conversation. Then he left, driving the vehicle past the gate.

"Anashe, did you notice anything strange at the gate five days ago when you came to pick up the bus?"

"I don't know what you're saying. What strange things?"

"Charm like things, spread by the gate?"

"It was a bit dark as dawn approached when I came. I couldn't notice anything. Why? Is it anything connected to what I'm suffering from?" He was out of breath. "Let's not get ahead of ourselves," he said.

"But let's not rule that out either. If that is the case, the person who put them there may have had an idea that you're likely to be the first to pass by the gate. If yes, someone who is against you in a way."

"If someone is against me, what is it they may not be happy with?"

Anashe looked at the roof in deep thought. "I can't think of anything but that I'm marrying you."

"So, you mean someone who may not like the fact that you and I are getting married?" said Tamara.

"Exactly," said Anashe.

"Anyone you think can be affected by this?" Tamara enquired.

"There was a lady by the name of Anamela who was my neighbour. She was more like my sister. She took good care of me. She'd cook and bring food for me. I'd help her also in keeping the same favour," said Anashe.

"Yes. But why do you think she can have anything to do with this charm issue?" Tamara asked.

"There's something I didn't tell you. She heard from my brothers that I'm planning to marry you. She confronted me and I innocently told her about my intentions with no suspicions," said Anashe.

"Uhuu… Then what?" asked Tamara.

"She didn't take it very well," Anashe said.

"But why?" asked Tamara.

"In her thinking, she anticipated that I'd consider marrying her because of her generosity towards me. I held no such intentions as I returned the favour innocently, but I guess she didn't share the same feelings," said Anashe.

"Still, it does not explain why you think she'd engage in witchcraft to deal with this matter," said Tamara.

"When I confronted her, she freaked out on me. It was a very unpleasant conversation and in conclusion, she warned me, saying she was going to do something to harm you or me," said Anashe.

"What? And you never told me?" said Tamara.

"I didn't want something upsetting you when all was merry, and moreover, I thought she was bluffing," said Anashe.

"No…" the word lagged as she spoke. "This is serious Anashe. This is very serious. I'll go and tell my grandfather right away so that he can advise what to do."

She left for home in a hurry. Tamara found her mother busy washing clothes outside. Her breathing was very fast as she was running home.

"Mother!"

"Yes, Tamara, you're breathless. Where are you coming from?"

"I went to see Anashe."

"Oh, how is he doing? He has failed to work for many days now," she said.

"Yes, mother. His health is deteriorating very fast, Mother. He has lost so much weight in the past few days."

"Oh, sorry. Is anyone taking care of him?" she asked.

"No, Mother. It's only when I go to see him that he even eats. He can't do much on his own. If no one goes there, he doesn't eat."

"We need to find a solution to this."

"But, Mother, there's something very serious I need to tell you."

"What, my daughter?"

Tamara frantically offloaded what Anashe had told her. Her mother saw the desperation in her watery eyes. Her body gesture had this tell-tell sign that communicated urgency in the matter. Her mother remembered her grandfather's words.

"Quickly, go and fetch your grandfather. Tell him to leave

everything he's doing and get here fast."

Tamara was already exhausted by the run from Anashe's place, but surprisingly still had strength to run to her grandfather's place. This time the strength came out of fear for Anashe's life. She entered grandfather's compound and found him relaxing under a mango tree.

"My granddaughter, how are you?"

"I'm well, Grandpa, but Mother says leave anything you're doing and urgently go to her."

"What has happened?"

"It's not her. Something is wrong with Anashe."

"Okay my daughter, let's go."

Tamara and her grandfather reached the Nkhosi's house. Mrs. Nkhosi was waiting at the entrance and received them quickly. As soon as she showed grandpa where to sit, she quickly dived into the subject.

"I think the results of the charms at the gate the other day have been revealed. Tamara, tell your grandfather what you just told me about Anashe."

She narrated the same story she told her mother to her grandfather about what Anashe had told her.

"I see. There's no other better reason but this. It makes so much sense that it's very serious."

"What are we going to do, then?" Mrs. Nkhosi asked grandpa.

"Tamara, you'll take me to Anashe's house and I'll see what can be done?"

Tamara and Grandpa left immediately for Anashe's place. He was fast asleep when the duo reached and knocked on his door. They had to knock several times until a noise was heard from inside. Then the door flung open.

"Come in." Anashe staggered and struggled to speak.

Tamara led the way as they entered.

The room was choking with a strange heat and sweat from the fever Anashe had. His body was boiling to an extent he was having blackouts. He nearly fell, trying to open the door. Tamara's grandfather was a prophet and detected the negative energy coming from Anashe. "You're right. Someone is not pleased with the move you've made to marry my granddaughter. I'll pray for the water and you drink it. Then continue to pray and I'll pray with you."

"Thank you, Grandpa." Anashe said.

"Now you, my dear will remain here to take care of him. He cannot be left alone. I'll tell your mother about his condition and that he can't be left alone," Grandpa instructed Tamara.

"Okay, Grandpa."

"See me out, daughter."

Outside the house, Tamara's grandfather spoke in an undertone to her.

"We need to let his family know about his condition. You'll leave when they send someone to take care of him."

"Yes, Grandpa."

Every day for one-week Grandpa would come to pray with Anashe and Tamara. Anashe had improved tremendously. When he was fully recovered, Anashe's brother set a date for marriage talks. They then got married after ten months in a wonderful wedding ceremony attended by family and friends.

Chapter 8

Tamara called out from the bathroom. "Honey, I've put the water on for you to bathe."

"I'll be there in a sec, sweetness" Anashe shouted from the bedroom as he packed his bag, preparing for a trip to South Africa. Six years had passed since their marriage and they had a daughter and another baby on the way. Tamara was heavy with a nine months old pregnancy.

"Is it a good idea for me to leave you in this condition? I can postpone the trip. What do you think?"

"Your customer says he needs this vehicle urgently. Just go, my sister is here with me. She will take care of me."

"Okay, I'll see that I get back quickly."

Before long, he was dressed and ready to go. They drove to Zambia's largest Bus Station, The Intercity Bus Terminus, and he boarded one of the Marcopolo buses heading to Cape Town. As he entered the bus, he was greeted by a man seated in the driver's seat. Anashe turned to eye the man talking, "Ah, Kaka, how are you?" extending his hand.

"I've been all right," Kaka responded.

"Are you the one driving us on this trip?"

"Yes, Anashe. Relax and make yourself comfortable. Kaka is in control," he prided himself.

"Okay, my seat number is somewhere in the middle there. Let me check it out, then I'll speak to you later.

"Okay, *boyi*," meaning friend.

"Halo Anashe," Mboozi, another of his friends was travelling on the same bus.

"I've not seen you in a long time. You've really put on some weight. My friend you need to start visiting the gym quite often," Anashe made fun of Mboozi.

"Stop with that teasing. You're making me feel uncomfortable," Mboozi protested as they laughed it away.

"Don't worry you look just as good as the last time I saw you."

"I hear you married, Anashe?

"Yes, I married this special lady. We were good friends for some time, then it developed into love for each other. I can say we understand each other very well. She's actually outside trying to find a parking space."

"I'm not seeing a ring on your finger, though."

"Mboozi, it's a long story."

"Give me a shorter version of it."

"Okay. I'll tell you about it as I wait for my wife."

"I went to South Africa about two years ago. You know, what we do renting an apartment and doing the catering on our own. I shared the room with Maimbo, you remember him?"

"Yes, I do. There was a trip I travelled with him about six months ago. We couldn't talk much as he was in the company of his brother and his brother's wife. He said they were going for a holiday or something like that."

"Yeah. We left our room late in the evening to buy some groceries to prepare supper. When leaving the store, we saw a lady putting on a mini skirt and high boots. She winked at me, trying to communicate something. I ignored her, seeing what she was wearing, concluded that she was a prostitute. We continued our journey, moving in zigzags as we always do when we are there crossing the road from one side to the other. When we were almost reaching the hotel, two men dressed in long black coats approached and showed us their guns belted in their waist. One had a flick knife and the other a wire that they sharpen and use to pierce through their victim's stomach up to the heart."

"Oh! That was tragic."

"Yes, tragic it was. Then we were asked to give them all our money. I remained with three hundred Rands in my pocket, got it and I gave it to them. I don't know exactly how much Maimbo gave them. Then he asked me to remove my wedding ring and give it to him. That's how I lost it and have not yet replaced it. I then reasoned that was why the lady with the short skirt winked at me. She was trying to warn me we were being followed by those thugs. She must have seen we were foreigners because it's easy for them to spot one."

"Sorry, my friend. As for me, I divorced Ezukanji and married this woman who is fourteen years older than me.

"*Eeeh*! That's serious."

"I married her for the money because I don't believe in love any more."

"Don't say that. I can challenge you. Love is real. How many children with Ezukanji?"

"Three. Two boys and a girl. She's my angel, Anashe. I miss her terribly."

"You see now that you've caused yourself so much pain by divorcing."

"I agree with you *boyi*. Otherwise, it's too late. I've already messed up."

"What led to the divorce?"

"You know I had always been a lady's man. A thing I'm now coming to realise was worthless. There's no happiness in that but trouble. She caught me red handed but up to now I still refuse the accusation, a thing that cost me my marriage."

"You can make good of that situation?"

"I don't think so, my friend. She hates me with a vengeance. She can never forgive me."

"Where is your seat?

"I'm seated at the back," Mboozi answered.

"Okay, we will catch up more later," Anashe announced.

Anashe settled in his seat and peered outside the window to eye Tamara. She had delayed trying to get the car well out of the way to the safety of the crowded station.

Anashe opened the window to have a clearer look as he spotted Tamara walking towards his window.

"You're all set to go now?" she inquired.

"Yes, and I've just discovered a colleague is driving us," he assured her.

"That's good. I'll be on my way now," as she walked the other direction while the bus eased on to the road from its parking lot.

Anashe took out a James Hadley Chase and began to read as the bus cruised at over a hundred kilometres per hour, leaving the busy traffic into the mountainous area. Before long, they reached the Chirundu border. They got off the bus to clear their passports and travelling documents. Passengers quickly refreshed themselves and bought some food for the distance ahead of them. As everyone took their seats, Anashe went to talk to Kaka. As they engaged in their talk, the conductor came to his window and handed him some bottles.

"Are those spirits?" Anashe inquired.

Kaka hesitated as he spoke. "Yes they are but…"

"Are you drinking and driving?"

"...No! I'm not. They're not mine. A friend has asked me to buy for him. He will soon join us on board."

As Kaka started the engine, Anashe went back to his seat and peered through the aisle to face Mboozi at the back.

"You can't believe Kaka has bought spirits, and I'm sure he wants to drink and drive."

"These guys are not serious. How can he do such a thing? We need to report him when we get to their office in South Africa. He can cause an accident and kill us." Mboozi complained.

"I'm just hoping he's telling the truth. The spirits are not his. Otherwise, when was the last time you went this side? I last went there a year ago."

"I was there just about a month ago." Mboozi said.

"How is the xenophobia situation going on there? I was discouraged to travel as I saw on social media the attacks there especially with our local drivers and others from foreign countries who were not allowed entry into South Africa. Those already in South Africa were being killed like dogs. It's terrible. People had their heads slashed with machetes," Anashe agonised.

"The one I just saw recently, one guy was being cut all over his body and blood was oozing out every part of him. The guy was in a pool of blood, cried for them to stop, but it was like those thugs were slashing grass. Another one I witnessed with my own eyes being burnt alive. They got a tyre and put it around him. Poured petrol and set him ablaze. I almost vowed never to go to South Africa again, but here I am travelling there. I guess I'm just stubborn."

"It's just that this is our livelihood. That's how we find ourselves going back there."

"Otherwise, look out for thieves who are drugging passengers," Mboozi warned.

"And how are they doing that?"

"They offer you something to eat or drink and they spike it with drugs. You go into a deep sleep then they search your pockets and bags to get whatever valuable items they find, especially money. Man, a lot of people have cried. This time around there's no playing Good Samaritan; you keep to your lane. Someone gives you a drink. You think it's sealed so it can't be drugged; you're making a big mistake. They use injections to administer the drug into the drink." Mboozi lectured.

"That's terrible. No association whatsoever. It's crazy."

They crossed the border into Zimbabwe and by this time the sun was about to set. Powerful red rays of the setting sun infiltrated the inside of the bus. Anashe got some sweets from his pocket and gave them to a little boy who was travelling with his parents to South Africa. The boy was very happy and he left his parents and sat with Anashe for a while before re-joining them.

Mboozi came through and spoke to the passenger who was seated next to Anashe.

"Excuse me brother, is it okay if we exchanged seats for a while? I want to talk to my brother here?"

"Not a problem at all. Where are you seated?"

"Seat number fifty-six, three rows behind."

The man squeezed past Anashe from the window side and Mboozi occupied Anashe's seat while he moved to where the man was seated.

"I was becoming bored behind there with ladies surrounding me. It's like the bus has been cut halfway with ladies occupying the back half."

"I didn't know that was the case." Anashe laughed.

"How is business?"

"Mboozi, I took a bit of a break after I was attacked while travelling back from there."

"You suffered another attack, Anashe?"

"Yes. I bought a minibus from one garage and started off for Zambia. I drove about thirty minutes on the highway to meet up with Chawezi, only to see a Volkswagen Golf trying to overtake. He pulled out a gun through the window and asked me to pull over. In the few seconds, I thought whether to do as was commanded or to continue. I just decided to speed off past them. They were on a chase after me and began to shoot. I stepped on the accelerator and the speedometer rose to one eighty on the clock. The VW golf came for me. I was driving a Toyota Hiace, and it seemed it was no match for the small car.

"My bus was pockmarked with bullets from the assailant's gun as he began to shoot. Both my rear and front windscreens were gone. I gave up and was almost coming to a stop. Then I saw Chawezi a few meters away from me. I gained courage and sped even further. As I neared to him, he heard the gun shots as they rang out. The repeated shots inundated the quiet mountainous road that was rather silent with echoes that Chawezi realised I was under attack. He was driving a Mitsubishi Canter and slowed down so I could go past him. At that time the Toyota Hiace minibuses were on demand from thieves in South Africa. When I was ahead of him, the VW Golf came for me, overtaking the Mitsubishi Canter. Chawezi tried to push the VW Golf out of the road by hitting on its side and blocking it on the right side to prevent it from reaching me. He created some space on the left side that allowed me to slow down and draw behind the Mitsubishi Canter.

"The VW Golf was now in front of the Mitsubishi Canter and I was behind it. We went on like that when the gunman aimed at me to just finish me off. He fired at me and hit the pillar of the minibus right on the side of my seat. I realised it was a matter of life and death here. I moved in front of the Mitsubishi Canter. They fired at Chawezi, missed him and the bullet went through the driver's window and right through the front windscreen shattering it completely. As the VW Golf came for me, I slowed down, giving it way to the front and went for its side. I hit it and it veered off the road. I only heard the squeaking of the tyres and saw a cloud of dust in the air. On the left side was a seemingly bottomless trench, as the road was on a mountainous place. Not knowing what had happened to the VW Golf, we sped off in our vehicles."

"Oh my God, that was serious."

"My dear Mboozi, if not for the strong pillar of the Hiace, I was going to be dead by now."

"You've had quite some experiences Anashe, *hee*."

"I've passed through thick and thin, my buddy. I'd have stopped going on these business trips if I didn't have the courage."

"I don't think I'd have gone back there after what you've just told me. It's like a clip from some action movie of sorts."

"When I reached the filling station and phoned my wife, she just said leave that thing and come back. Ha ha ha," Anashe laughed.

"Finding myself in her position, I'd have said the same thing. You know, you can buy another vehicle, but you can't buy life."

"Yeah! Then on another trip, I left South Africa, drove about one thousand two hundred kilometres. I did another seven hundred kilometres in Botswana came to a game park and noticed two trucks parked side by side. The drivers were tired and decided to take a rest. I was also very sleepy and thought of taking a rest myself. Since I was now not alone, I felt safe and parked in between the trucks, as there was enough space. Around four a.m., I woke up to find the trucks gone. I didn't hear them leave but they were not there. I looked in the side mirror and saw a light behind the car. I was startled, unsure where the light was coming from as I didn't see any vehicle behind me. I gunned the engine of the car and sped off in fear. As I drove, I imagined it was a ghost and I really hit the road in extreme nervousness. The Corolla sped almost hitting the limit of the speedometer. In no time, I reached the border. When I had relaxed, I quizzed myself about what I saw. I then realised that when I slept, I leaned on the steering wheel and stepped on the brakes. When I woke up and looked in the mirror, it was the brake lights I saw on and I didn't think about that."

Mboozi burst into laughter. "*Boyi*, you were running away from yourself, *eh*?"

"You can imagine. It's funny now, but it was not then. The fear of seeing a ghost."

They both laughed loudly, attracting attention from the passengers around them.

As Mboozi's laughter died down, he said, "As for me, I've had fewer encounters like yours which seem life threatening."

"It's just God who keeps us, you know. Every trip is a new encounter, and anything can happen. These ones I've told you are very significant in my life, but there're more."

"Tell me at least one last one. You're really tickling me with these stories while others are teaching me how to react if I find myself in a similar situation. It was actually brave of you to react like you did in a life-threatening situation."

"Ah *boyi*, we shall chat later."

"No. Just one last one *boyi*. Another funny one, if possible."

"Okay, okay, you win. This one, I drove in the park. It's a pity that if you get tired, you need to rest otherwise you can cause an accident. When I got tired, I took risks in the past, to sleep anywhere as long as I didn't come out of the car. This time I slept in a park, then woke up around three a.m. and was about to start off. I started the engine and ran the car for a few minutes. I was so pressed because I took a lot of water just before I parked the previous night. I looked around, didn't see anything, then I decided to relieve myself.

"I left the engine running, the car in neutral and lights on in readiness for any eventualities then went out of the car. I left the door open just in case, I could run back and enter the car with ease. I went to a nearby tree and began relieving myself. I then heard activity in front of the car. Bellows of dust rose in front of the high beam lights which had attracted animals. I saw a hyena pass by with its tail tucked in. Before long I saw a lion chasing after it. I ran to the car for safety. In a panic trying to enter the car, I bumped in the door and it closed on me."

"Ooh dame!" Mboozi exclaimed, locking his hands on his head in trepidation.

"Yes *boyi*, I was so panicked that instead of opening the door, I entered through the window. It was three quarters open, and I dived in. The small space of the window that was up caught the buckle of my belt. I couldn't move. My legs were outside up to my waist waving in the air while the other half was inside with my head-first."

"Hahaha. You're killing me." Mboozi was laughing loudly again. He laughed so deep a cough came out of him.

"Don't choke yourself, man. I haven't even finished."

"You're killing me, *boyi*." He went on laughing and coughing.

"Let me finish *boyi*, otherwise I'll end here."

"Okay, I've stopped. He held his mouth to stop it from bursting into another round of laughter. Finish up my guy."

"All right. As I went in head-first, my right hand went for the gear level while my left went for the hand brake for grip. I don't know if I should say I was fortunate enough, I pressed the hand brake button and released the brake as I pushed on it with my weight. And in pulling on the gear, it moved to drive, and the car was propelled into motion. It started moving slowly and my legs waved wildly in the air for some balance. The hyena noticed the car moving, and it crossed back, running in the direction it came. The lion followed and came to the right side where I was, stood in utter surprise when my legs went past its mouth as it ducked them. *Boyi*, I was going to be eaten clean. I've never been so afraid in my life. My chest was burning. I felt like fire was coming out of my mouth from fear. The lion just stood there watching while I panicked. I counted myself one of the lucky *chaps* around."

"You're really lucky my friend. So, how did you stop the car?"

"I let it move a distance as I struggled to free my buckle off the window. Luckily, the area was clear, no obstacles in front. Then I pulled myself into the car, turned in the passenger's seat, stepped on the brake, pressed the window button to raise them, then pushed the gear to park for a while. I looked back only to see the baby hyena caught up in the mouth of the same lion I passed. It hit my thoughts that it could have been my legs in the mouth of that vicious lion. I then put the car in drive again and sped off. Some life encounters are something else."

"Yeah man, they're quite something. Tell you what, your children, especially grand children need to hear about them.

They'll learn some survival skills."

It had become dark and the wind whistled as it entered the open windows of the bus. After enjoying the chat with Mboozi, Anashe looked out the window to view the Zimbabwean terrain. They passed through some towns and Anashe entertained himself by watching the houses and building around in the night light. How the small dots of light sparkled in the distant view of approaching cities. Anashe started dozing, and he covered himself with a blanket for his long sleep while making the cross-trip through Zimbabwe. At this point, they were coming from Chegutu crossing in the mountainous area of Kadoma rural, a mining town. He was irritated by a certain company of guys speaking a foreign language. They were chattering and mumbling loudly, laughing all the way as they spoke. Fortunately, Anashe managed to get some sleep.

He was suddenly woken up by the screeching of the tyres as Kaka was braking to reduce the speed of the bus. He had driven around a mountain at high speed only to appear tailing a slow-moving car. Kaka frantically tried to reduce the speed preventing himself from hitting the car, but he couldn't. He decided to overtake the car, but on the outer side of the road was a mountain and so turned to the inner right lane for oncoming vehicles. His judgement was impaired by the alcohol he had taken while driving. He could not manage to go past the car as there was an oncoming truck also at full speed. He then decided to cut across the road to the outer side of the road. As he crossed the right lane, Anashe rose to his feet to witness what was happening as passengers screamed for their lives. Accident! accident! The truck hit the middle of the bus as it tried to squeeze its way past it and on the other side electricity pole lines. The impact of the truck into the bus was heavy and noisy, like a bomb.

"Accident! accident!" more screams were heard from the passengers.

The bus was pushed into the electricity pole lines, which produced violent sparks and went up in flames.

"Hoow! Hoow! Help! help!" they yelled as the bus was lifted in the air.

Anashe turned to face the rear and went for the exit window at the back as he held tightly to the rail. The bus went flying and hit the ground on its right side with a loud and heavy thud. Windows broke and seats were uprooted from their screws and piled up on one side of the bus, trapping the travellers all on one side, including Anashe who was now knocked down. As the bus began to slide on its side on the ground, it left openings through which the passengers went through, and the bus went over them grinding and cutting their limbs. Some had their legs, hands or ears ripped off, while others had their torsos frayed and others fell out completely and the bus slid over them, killing them on the spot.

As Anashe was sent to the side of the bus, his hand protruded from the window and it was dragged on the road as he was pressed by other passengers. His hand tore with a large laceration from his lower hand passed the elbow and all the way to his upper arm that exposed the bones. Blood oozed profusely and he became frail. (The hand ultimately survived amputation because he was wearing a leather jacket.) When the bus came to a halt, Anashe rose and reached for the exit window behind the bus. Dust entered the bus, making passengers look like shadows. It made it difficult for them to recognise and see each other. Anashe stepped on the window, pushing it with all the energy he could gather. A strong wind blew, sweeping the inside of the bus and blowing some of the dust out. There was some illumination inside the bus as a result of the broken exit window. Passengers rushed for the exit. As they made their way, the stepped on the injured ones. As Anashe was about to go through the window, a voice called from behind him.

"Uncle, Uncle, help me," the little boy called out as his parents collapsed due to pain and blood loss and were buried in the luggage and chair piles. They both had one leg each cut off.

Anashe reached out and pulled the boy as he could not move due to a seat that crushed on him. As Anashe pulled the boy completely out of the bus, he noticed he only had one hand and blood all over him on the left side where the hand was torn off. Anashe quickly wrapped the boy's hand with a cloth he pulled from the pile of luggage and secured the blood flow.

"Hey, Mister, can you take care of this boy as we wait for an ambulance," Anashe spoke as he gave the boy to one of the onlookers from a nearby village who had started gathering around the bus.

He then put pressure over his own tear in the hand to stop himself from losing a lot of blood. At this time, he was feeling dizzy from the blood loss and he sat down. He started having blurred vision, seeing people as silhouettes. As he turned on the other side, he saw luggage and dead bodies that were thrown out of the bus lay scattered on the road while others were trapped inside the bus. He recognised most of the people as he chatted with some of them on the bus. Limbs of passengers were all over the road. His body was aching everywhere. He was bruised and his garments tattered. A big hole on the left side of his bum cheeks was exposing a big graze, very deep, that was bleeding and felt cold on the rest of his trousers.

He was now sliding into and out of consciousness. One helper with a van was quickly ordered by a police officer, who had reached the accident scene earlier than any medical help, to carry the critical ones. Anashe was among the first to be rushed to the nearest hospital As he was helped inside the van, he called out to the onlookers for the boy that was hurt. They quickly looked for him and handed the boy over to him. Anashe placed him in between his legs to secure him for the trip. Other, more critical ones who could not travel in the van had to wait for ambulances. This caused word to reach hospitals nearby, and they began sending ambulances to the accident scene.

Chapter 9

The first hospital they reached, Kadoma General Hospital, had no facilities to handle emergencies like the casualties that came in. It lacked an ambulance to transport the accident victims to another, bigger hospital. A good Samaritan volunteered to transport them in a Toyota Venture. The journey to the next hospital was about an hour and was agonizing. The car was cruising at above 140 kilometres per hour on an uneven pebble road. Anashe and the other casualties were screaming in pain due to the vibration of the vehicle.

"If I slow down so that you don't feel a lot of pain means I'll be killing you because you're all bleeding and you need to be quickly attended to. It's better you feel pain now, but you survive," the driver of the Venture, a military man, advised.

At this point, Anashe felt as though he was dying. When he was conscious, he had pain all over his body. When he slipped into unconsciousness, an empty darkness overshadowed him. He felt very light as though he had left his body. Then after a few minutes he'd open his eyes to the reality of the bumpiness and painful journey. The five casualties reached the general hospital and were received by three male doctors and four nurses. Three operating room tables were wheeled quickly to the Toyota Venture. Anashe was one of the first casualties to be wheeled on the patient trolley into the hospital casualty ward. One doctor was pulling Anashe's trolley while a nurse was pushing it. They passed through a long corridor and entered a large room. Anashe opened his eyes to a strong beam of light shining over him, it blinded his view.

The anaesthesiologist in the theatre was in an operating room scrub suit, a face mask and its matching hat. A stethoscope hung around his neck and he hurriedly began taking Anashe's vitals. He pulled the anaesthesia cart and instruments trolley closer to himself. Another surgeon, also in operating room scrubs began running intravenous fluids to replace the much lost water and blood. Once they were flowing smoothly, the surgeon prepared his operating instruments. The two doctors began asking Anashe about the accident while another gave him an injection. As he explained, he began to feel drowsy and his voice slurred until eventually he passed out.

"This laceration is deep and dirty. It needs thorough cleaning. Open this flap so the debris can come out."

"Certainly, Doctor!"

"Okay, here we go. Hold the hand firmly, but give me some room."

"Noted, Doctor."

Three hours had passed since Anashe had entered the theatre. The two doctors were still concentrated on the operation. A female nurse stood by, watching the surgeons and the readings on the monitor.

"The lower hand doesn't look good either. Seems it has a fracture. I need an X-ray taken to confirm this," the surgeon suggested.

At that instant Anashe mumbled something and raised his hand to pull out the IVs. The surgeon gazed at the anaesthesiologist.

"Are you sure you gave him the right dose? Why is he awake?" the surgeon snapped.

"Yes, I'm certain I gave him the right dose." He hesitated in his response.

"Are you sure or not? Give him another dose. I'm not done here."

The anaesthesiologist hastily picked up another IV and administered it.

After some hours, Anashe woke up in the ward, his head and hand bandaged and other wounds and bruises cleaned. He looked around the room but didn't see any familiar faces. A nurse passed by his bed and showed Anashe an X-ray that revealed his left hand was broken.

"Nurse, I came with a small boy around ten years of age, sustained an amputated left hand. Could you tell me where he is and how he's doing?"

"What's his name?"

"I don't know. I came with him that's why I'm asking after him. I don't know the fate of his parents."

"I'll check for him in the children's ward."

Anashe and other victims who had been brought in by ambulances were hospitalised to stabilise them, while the rest who were not hurt were discharged.

"Halo Chawezi. Mboozi here!"

"We've just had an accident and your friend Anashe is in critical condition."

"Anashe was in an accident?"

"Yes, Chawezi. He's not doing very well."

"Are you sure he's alive?"

"Yes, he is, but I don't know for how long he will hang on. He was bleeding badly when he was brought to the hospital. I had to follow him to ensure he was attended to. Since yesterday, he has been to theatre three times now. You need to come quick. Conditions here are not too good. There's no water and people are taking advantage of us selling water at two hundred United States dollars. Food is also very expensive. The money that we have will not sustain us if we delay too much."

"What really happened? How did the accident happen?" Chawezi inquired.

"Actually, Anashe's the one who saw that the driver, Kaka, remember him? had bought alcohol and was drinking while driving."

"How come Anashe allowed that to happen? Because, knowing his pragmatism, he would not allow it. He's not keen on such misconducts."

"The guy said the spirits were for his friend who was to come on board somewhere in Zimbabwe. Anashe doubted but didn't pursue the issue further."

"Ooh, that's sad. And you, how are you?"

"I only have minor injuries, so have been discharged. I'm waiting to see how they ferry him back to Zambia. You must inform his family."

"Okay, I will, but make sure he's taken good care of. If it's bills, I'll come and deal with them when I travel there."

"Come in Chawezi, you're welcome," Tamara sounded still very sore from childbearing as she had only given birth to her second child two days ago.

"You've come to see the new addition to the Ncube family?"

"May I see that newcomer? Bring her here. Wow, she's a big baby. We welcome you to this world," Chawezi tried to sound calm.

"Can I offer you a drink or some water?" said Tamara.

"Some cold water will do, thanks?" he replied.

As she came back from the kitchen and placed the glass of water on the table, Chawezi began to speak.

"Tamara, aside from seeing the baby I've come for another matter. I've some bad news but there's hope too. The bus which Anashe travelled in was involved in an accident in Zimbabwe."

Tamara felt her heart pump blood fast in the veins of her head and light flashed in her eyes. She could feel her anxiety levels rising and sucking the air out of her lungs. She felt like she was going to collapse.

"What did you say?" Her voice sounded as though she spoke in slow motion.

"Anashe was in an accident," Chawezi echoed.

"Tell me the truth. Is Anashe alive or dead?" Tamara demanded with a voice that quivered with fear.

"He's definitely alive, but he's critical. Someone needs to travel to Zimbabwe to attend to all his needs. I'm told water is a problem there so there's a need to continue buying it for washing the wounds in theatre and for drinking. I'd have wanted you to accompany me on the trip, but you can't with a two days old baby."

"If you're telling me the truth, yes I'd have wanted to be with him right now. I know he needs me now in his condition, but the baby needs me the most," Tamara said in a grouchy tone as she felt a lump in her throat and a cramp in her stomach, like labour pains.

"I know it's a difficult decision for you, but it's for the best. I'll travel with his brother tomorrow morning and we'll keep you informed," Chawezi stressed.

"God will go before you and He'll take care of Anashe."

In the solitude of the dark, as Tamara lay on her bed, she sobbed quietly, thinking how Anashe must be suffering. Is he going to survive or not?

"If the worst happened, how will I keep the children?" she asked herself.

She prayed for him ardently and slid into sleep.

Chawezi walked the aisles of the hospital from end to end, went back again. Just as he was giving up, a voice spoke in a weak tone.

"Chawezi, I'm here," Anashe breathed heavily as he spoke, almost like draining the air out of himself.

Chawezi went closer to inspect with incredulity while he was looking at his friend.

"It's me you're looking at my friend, its I Anashe,"

His head still in bandages was swollen to a size that indicated possible broken skull. Scratch marks all over his head and face, a broken right incisor tooth. A large and deep tear on his left palm that opened and closed like an envelope. Anashe was without clothing, only some pants and the leather coat as the other clothes were ripped in the accident.

"You sound like Anashe all right, but you don't look like him, my friend. What happened?" Chawezi was horrified.

"Chawezi it was terrible. I almost died. You remember kaka the cross-border driver?"

"Yes, I remember him."

"He was the one who was driving us, and he drank while driving. I confronted him, but he refuted it. Then, as we entered Zimbabwe his driving became very bad. He was speeding and ended up with wrong judgement. He avoided hitting a slow-moving car and decided to cross the road. He didn't manage to avoid the oncoming truck and it hit the belly of the bus. The impact sent the bus sliding on the road, chopping our limbs, people's heads in the process. It was bad my friend."

"I've noticed Mboozi is peeping from the flash doors of the ward. Yes, he's traumatised to see you in that condition. There he is. Mboozi come in! Anashe's here, come!" Chawezi shouted to him. Mboozi was still standing at the entrance, holding on to the doors, not finding courage to enter the ward.

"He seems not to be ready to see you," said Chawezi

"Leave him, I understand his trauma," Anashe said.

"How is my family? I heard my wife gave birth to a baby girl. How is she? How is my wife doing?"

"Your wife is taking the message with calmness. She couldn't come because of the baby."

"Chawezi, it's better that she's there than here. Who will take care of the children and run my home? It's better that way."

"I've come with your young brother and he'll soon join us. I left him at the front desk enquiring about you."

"Thanks for coming, Chawezi." Anashe gratified his friend.

"Don't mention it my friend. You'd have done the same if I were in your position. What are we to do now?"

"You need to make arrangements to take me back home."

"Excuse me, doctor." Chawezi was rushing to a doctor who was attending to all the victims of the accident.

"I meant to inquire over the decision of one of the victims in the road traffic accident that happened two days ago coming from Zambia."

"What can I help you with, sir," the doctor responded.

"I wanted to know if he can be moved as I want to arrange to ferry him back home to Zambia."

"We are in talks with the transporter and their insurance company to deal with all eventualities, including ferrying the patients back home. Some of them can't travel by road but by air. This will be done collectively, so you wait. I'll brief you on the outcome," the doctor assured.

"Thank you so much doctor. I shall wait for your advice."

Anashe could not get to sleep, and he entered into meditation. It came back to him that a few months ago he was in a service in church where his pastor prophesied to him that a trap had been set for an accident on his way to his usual business trips in the mountains of Zimbabwe. The spiritual father told him not to go until after three months had passed. Anashe heeded that warning and only travelled after a year.

"I guess that is why I'm alive. God has spared me. Maybe if I had travelled in the three months, I was going to die," he mumbled to himself.

"Thank you, Lord, I thank you."

Five days later, Anashe and twenty-one others touched down at Lusaka International airport in a Boeing 747. After all passengers exited the plane, the patients were wheeled into the first aid emergency room. After being cleared, families of the patients who came to receive them were allowed in before being transported to the University Teaching Hospital.

Tamara entered the emergency room to look for Anashe. She went past a few patients with missing ears, hands or legs, or a combination of all. It was a sorry sight. She prepared herself for the worst, as she went on searching now making a return trip to where she started from. Anashe called for her.

"Tamara, I'm here."

She could not recognise him as he was still swollen and the outfit he was now wearing was unfamiliar to her. He was wearing Chawezi's clothes. They looked oversize on him as Chawezi was short and portly. She came closer and inspected him.

"How are you my husband?" Tamara was about to hug Anashe.

"No, no, no, my love. Please don't. You're going to hurt me."

"Okay love, sorry."

"By God's grace, I'm much better. The pains that I feel now can't be compared with what I went through just after the accident. How is my newly born baby?"

"She's well."

"And the elder sister?"

"They're both well."

"I want to see my children. Bring them to the hospital."

"I can only bring the older one."

Tamara could only see the right hand. Thinking the let hand had been amputated, she thanked God, and sighed with relief as a thought ran through her mind.

"I hear they're preparing you to go to University Teaching Hospital?"

"Yes dear. Our wounds were just being cleaned; we've not even started treatment as it is. There're a lot of things to be done."

A few minutes later, a doctor made his way into the Airport Emergency Room.

"How are the patients doing? My name is Doctor Thabo Mwanamuke. Okay now, visitors leave us to prepare the patients for exit. They need to be rushed to hospital," he stated as he started attending to them.

"How is it in there? Did you find Anashe?" Tamara's elder sister asked.

"Yes. I found him," she said, looking distraught, her mind a jumble.

"What's the condition like in there?" her sister probed further.

"Looks like his left hand was amputated, and he has grazes on the head and face. He looks better than most of them I've seen." Tamara added.

"Sister, thank God he's alive."

"Yes, sister, you're right. We need to go prepare some soup for him and follow them to the hospital."

They left the airport in the escort of Police motor bikes and cars to ward off traffic as the Marcopolo bus they were in turned ambulance. Family members also followed the convoy, causing a traffic jam.

It was busy at the University Teaching Hospital Casualty bay as the bus arrived, doctors and nurses were waiting to receive the survivors and attend to the them. Media was everywhere reporting on the accident as narrated by the victims. Anashe was one such victim who was conscious and could be interviewed by the reporters. The national television monitored a clip of the victims' arrival at International airport as well as the hospital as breaking news. Most of the casualties were on stretcher trolleys, as some didn't have limbs and others were still unconscious. A separate ward was reserved for the accident victims who were in critical condition. Some went directly to theatre to have their wounds further worked on. Others suffered amputation as gangrene began its attack. A team of Zambian doctors and government officials were dispatched to investigate the accident and help attend to the patients who could not be moved from hospital in Zimbabwe.

Tamara entered the ward with some food for Anashe in a small basket. As Anashe prepared to eat, he moved himself to settle on the bed. It was then that Tamara discerned he actually had both his hands only that he could not fit in the shirt's arm because of the bandage on his hand. He had his shirt buttoned all the time because he was still feeling feverish.

"I thought your left hand was cut off?" Tamara said.

"No, it's there, but it's seriously injured. I don't know if it'll survive amputation," Anashe said.

"God will not allow you to lose your hand," Tamara assured. "Don't worry, the doctors and I will take care of it."

After feeding, Anashe's elder brother remained tending to him. As he slept, he kept replaying the vision of the accident and each time would fall off the bed. This happened three times until the nurse on duty said, "bring down the mattress from the bed and allow the patient to sleep on the flat floor, otherwise he's going to break himself. We can't restrict him to the bed as of one who has lost his mind."

As he settled in the hospital, he started healing very well and the wounds closed up. Some of his friends were discharged while others died in hospital. He called the nurse in Zimbabwe to find out the fate of the small boy. He was informed that the boy had missed his parents as they were taken to South Africa for treatment while he remained in Zimbabwe. They later reunited when the boy could be transported. Anashe was very happy to hear the good news.

Chapter 10

He looked at the image that was reflecting back at him from a full-length mirror and he was scared at what he saw. His scratched head and face, his mutilated hand and broken tooth disfigured him. Anashe was discharged from hospital after a month and was now at home

"Is this what happened to me? This is bad. I'm no longer as handsome as I was. Will I be able to use my hand again?" There was sombreness in his complaining.

He stayed in hospital the last month without knowing how he looked. He was so swollen he couldn't turn his head to see the back of his hand. He requested a mirror a number of times, to be brought to the hospital so he could see his wounds, but Tamara purposely ignored his requests. She didn't want him to see the open laceration that showed even the movement of bones as he stretched and folded his hand. She feared him becoming depressed.

"My husband, you're doing fine now. You were very bad when you first arrived back home from Zimbabwe. I was not sure of your survival. The doctors are commending your healing process, so you can't despair now. Instead, you must thank our good Lord for being alive and remember you'll always be handsome to me." She smiled warmly at him.

He tried to smile, but his face was blank and cold.

"I was relieved when I thought only your left hand had been ripped off, but seeing you still had every part of you intact was gratifying. You're still who I married, after all."

The hand still needed a lot of healing that was to take at least eighteen months. The veins and muscles in the hand had been severed and needed to grow again for Anashe to be able to use his hand. During the cleaning of his wound, debris and broken glass came out of it that made Tamara unnerved. She prayed this glass would not travel in the blood stream and reach Anashe's heart. Tamara helped Anashe with his physiotherapy sessions to help him use his hand again. A year later, the open wound healed after being grafted with skin from his thigh. He underwent surgery and plates were put in his left hand to support the broken bone.

Fadzai came to see Anashe after he had been discharged.

"How are you doing, my son?"

"I'm much better, Papa. I've improved quicker than the doctors had anticipated."

"How come you follow me in almost all happenings in your life? Do you remember that I've plates on the ulna bone of the same hand as yours that I sustained from a mechanical accident? And you've had yours in a motor accident."

"Yes, Father, I remember."

"I hope none of your sons walk your path of pain and suffering, my son."

"I pray God will break some of the generation curses in my family."

Anashe extended his hand and squeezed his father's hand tightly.

"The God that allowed us to live will guide and keep them as well."

At this time, Anashe and Tamara's family had grown to three

children when God appeared in Tamara's dreams again. In her dream, she was laying in her bed. The room was dark as in the night. Suddenly, a shooting star came down from the sky with a loud noise and shone luminously through the window into her bedroom. She was startled and came out of bed with stupendous speed. Swiftly Tamara went to peer by the window just as it passed to drop the other side of the house. She darted to the self-contained bathroom, propped herself by the bathtub and gazed outside the small window. It hit the ground with an explosion, left a hole and went off, plunging the place into darkness again. As Tamara was still bolstered and scanning the area, she switched her attention to crying voices she heard coming from the direction of the gate. She quickly ran outside to inquire what was going on. She swung the gate on its roller wheels, opening it with so much energy. For a moment, she stood there petrified and her heart raced at discovering it was her mother and sisters.

"Mother, why are you crying?" she mouthed desperately. "Answer me, Mother!" She shook her vigorously, all to no avail. She turned to her sisters. "*Sisi*, what's the matter? Why are you all crying?"

"Daddy is dead."

"What? Why are you saying that?"

"Yes, *sisi*. Daddy is dead."

Her body jerked at the information as though hit by a flying object. She pressed herself to hug her sister tight, and she also burst into a loud sob. Tamara joined them and led them into the yard.

At that point, Anashe noticed her groaning and moaning in her fitful sleep. He shook her to snap her out of it. As she woke up, Tamara continued to cry loudly.

"What's the matter, Tamara?" Anashe asked in a panic.

"Speak to me, Tamara, please, have I done something wrong?"

She didn't respond, instead put a refraining hand to Anashe motioning for him to wait. After a few minutes, she finally was calm, and she began to narrate her vision to a desperate Anashe.

"I sure hope this turns out to be just a nightmare. Your father will be just fine." Anashe tried to comfort her.

She woke up and readied herself to go for work. She sat in the tub and ran the water. She sat there staring at the water in the bath tub as though she was seeing something inside it. It was as if the noisy running water from the tap hypnotised her. She pondered on her dream and, snapping out of her hypnosis, discovered the tub was almost running over. She quickly turned off the tap and resolved to visit her father before going to the office.

The place was quiet when Tamara entered her father's house. Her aunties, sisters to her father had come from the village to see him when they heard his high blood pressure had worsened. He was having blackouts from time to time.

"Where is Father?" Tamara asked, trying to conceal her fears.

"He's in the bathroom," one of her aunties responded.

"I've come to see him before I go to the office. How is he doing now?"

"He's better now. You're supposed to be at the office, aren't you working?"

"I'm , Aunty, I just wanted to see Father before I go."

Tamara's father walked into the living room in a pair of shorts. His knees looked swollen from the gout he was suffering from.

"Morning, Daddy. How are you feeling after the medication you were given by the doctor?"

"Better dear. The swelling has lessened, but the pain is still there."

"I've come to pray with you, and I'd like to invite you to my church this coming Sunday."

"Not a problem, dear."

They prayed together and Tamara took her anointing oil and anointed her father on the head, face and the hands through to his legs. On Sunday, Tamara picked her father up and they went to church. After the sermon, the pastor began to prophesy.

"I see an elderly man going to the grave. If it's the will of God that he be taken, we've no authority to overrule. However, we ask that God have mercy on him and heal him."

At testimony time, Tamara rose and went to the pulpit.

"I believe that the prophesy you've just given is my father's. I had a vision this week on Tuesday that he had passed. I understood God's communication, and I went to pray for him. I then invited him to church, and he's seated in the pew over there."

"Father, come to the front. I pray for you," the pastor called on him.

"Bring him a chair, as he's finding it difficult to stand for too long," Tamara advised.

The pastor prayed and requested that seven bottles of water be bought for him. He prayed over them and asked him to drink one every day starting that very day. As they drove home, Tamara thought about the whole episode; the dream she had and now the prophecy and decided on a very important matter. They reached home and found her mother there. As her father and she settled down, she laid her gift on the table and popped a request.

"Father and Mother, I'm asking for your blessing?"

"Of course, my dear, we shall bless you."

They both spoke words to Tamara and blessed her with a

prayer.

Monday the next day, his sisters left for the village after staying for a month. When they left, Mr. Nkhosi appeared to be dejected. During that same week on Wednesday, he insisted that he also travel to the village to refresh his mind.

"Daddy, you're not well enough to travel. Your sisters have just left for the village. Why would you be travelling there also?" Tamara quizzed.

"Leave me be. I want to get some fresh air."

"Okay. Since we can't stop you, travel safely and take care of yourself."

Mr. Nkhosi left the following day on Thursday. He confirmed his reaching the village.

The sisters were astonished at his showing up unannounced as they had just left his home, but they didn't want to chastise him.

"You're here, brother. You're welcome. What brings you here just after we left your home?"

"I just want to refresh myself. I've stayed in the house for too long."

"Okay brother. You're welcome."

"We know we were at your home four days ago, but how have you been?"

"I'm doing much better now."

He booked himself into a lodge to avoid crouching when visiting the pit latrine. His knees were still sore. In the morning, he'd go to the village and spend the whole day there only to come back in the evenings. That Sunday three days after his arrival, he went to watch some soccer at a nearby village. Village teams were competing in a tournament for some prize money. In the afternoon, he didn't feel well and asked to be taken back to his room. His nephew drove him to the lodge and left him there.

The late afternoon breeze as the sun began to set poured over the wet lawn outside, sweeping into his room. He felt nauseated. He went outside the room and threw up. One of the gardeners came to check on him.

"Excuse me, sir, are you all right?" he asked.

"I'll be fine my son. I just felt a bit nauseous, otherwise it's nothing serious."

"Okay, sir. Let me know if you need some help."

"Thank you, son," he responded with a few words, letting out a burp as he tried not to enter another wave of vomit. He wiped his mouth with the back of his hand awkwardly.

He entered his room and left the door open to allow fresh air in. After two hours, the same gardener who saw Mr. Nkhosi earlier happened by his room and noticed the door still open. At this time, it had started to get dark and mosquitoes were entering his room. He meant to warn Mr. Nkhosi to close his door as he peeped through.

"Hallo! Hallo, sir!" he shouted. "Sir, are you there? Your door is open and mosquitoes are going in. Sir!"

When there was no response, he entered the room. Then he came to the bed area, but there was no one there. He knocked at the bathroom door that was also ajar, but there was no one there either. He went back in the room and looked on the other side of the bed. As he proceeded, he noticed human feet appearing, then the legs, before he could see the entire body. He realised Mr. Nkhosi had collapsed on the floor.

"Sir, are you okay?" He shook him by the legs, but he was not responding. He ran to reception to report the incident.

"Madam, the elderly man I told you about who was vomiting a while ago has collapsed in his room."

Without waiting for further explanation, the receptionist quickly ran to Mr. Nkhosi's room as the gardener trailed behind her. While in the room, they tried to revive him, but to no avail. She went back to reception and made a call to the owner of the lodge.

The phone rang about four times before it was answered.

"Madam, we've a guest who has passed out in his room. He's not responding. We need to take him to a medical facility."

"*Hee!* What exactly do you mean by 'he has collapsed?'"

"Yes mum, he is as dead on the floor."

"Oh my, I'm on my way coming there." The madam responded in disbelief.

She arrived quickly, her face in panic as she scurried to Mr. Nkhosi's room.

"Give way please. How is he?"

"Mum, he's not responding."

"Help me," she told the receptionist. "Quick, hold him by the legs, Masauso, hold him in his armpits." The madam further ordered. "I'll hold his back." They lifted him to the car that was parked right outside the room. The car screeched as it nosed outside the gate onto the main road and sped off. The receptionist kept her vigil at Mr. Nkhosi all the time calling out his name. On their way, before they reached the hospital, Mr. Nkhosi opened his eyes, breathed a deep breath and a croaking sound escaped his throat, and then closed his eyes again.

"Mum, he's dead!" the receptionist yelled.

"Oh my God. Are you sure?" the madam was shaking on the steering wheel.

"Yes, madam. He's not breathing!" she said in a sobbing,

high-pitched voice.

"Calm down. Let's not get ahead of ourselves. Let the doctors determine that."

At the Hospital Police Post, the policeman in charge reported him brought in dead. The police asked if he had a mobile phone on him. The lodge receptionist handed it to them. They scrolled until they found a number saved under 'wife'.

The policeman dialled the number and an elderly voice came on the other side.

"Hallo."

"Hallo, madam. I'm calling you from the General Hospital Police Post. I'm Sergeant Soko. Do you know a Mr. Nkhosi?" the officer inquired.

"Yes, I do. He's my husband."

"Do you know where he is?"

"He left on Thursday for Chipata."

"Where are you, madam?"

"I'm in Lusaka."

"Oh, okay. Is that where you live with him?"

"Yes. He went to visit his family at the village. Why are you asking me these questions?"

"Madam, are you aware that your husband was booked at a lodge here in Chipata?"

"Yes. Because he has problems with his legs, so he opted to sleep at a lodge rather than at the village. May I know why I'm answering these questions?"

"Sorry, mum, to deliver this news in this manner but your husband has just passed away on his way to the hospital. He fell sick while in his room and as they were rushing him to the hospital, we lost him. Kindly let your relatives come and positively identify him at Chipata General Hospital before we take him to the morgue."

Mrs. Nkhosi was confused after receiving the news of her husband's death. She immediately called the nephew who had taken him to the lodge earlier.

"Peter, where are you?"

"I've just come from leaving Uncle and was watching soccer at the next village."

"I've just received a call that your uncle is dead."

"No. How come? I think there's some sort of mistake. I'm just from leaving him at the lodge. He wasn't that bad, though he complained of not feeling too well."

"Get there quickly and confirm what the police officer was saying. He said you go to Chipata Central Police, then he'll take you to the General Hospital to identify the body."

After concluding his conversation, the nephew went on to deliver the bad news to his family.

"Aunty, I've just received a call from Aunty in Lusaka, that Uncle whom I've left at the lodge has just died."

"Hey! Don't say that. What do you mean? We said our goodbyes not long ago to your uncle. How can he be dead?"

"That's what Aunty has said. She's also not sure, so let's go and check just to rest our curiosity."

The trio arrived at the Police Station. The reception area was swarming with people who brought in two gentlemen covered in blood. They were involved in a fight over debt and were still arguing.

"Excuse us, excuse." They made their way to a policeman at the desk who was attending to the visitors.

"Excuse us, sir, we are here to see Sergeant Soko."

"That's me. How can I help you?"

"We're here in connection with Mr. Nkhosi's case. I received a call from Lusaka saying that I needed to identify a man who was brought in dead."

"Oh, yes! The owner of the lodge where he was staying came and gave a report of his demise. Is this his registration card?"

"Yes, it is."

"So, these are his personal effects?"

"Yes officer."

"Let's go to the mortuary so you can identify him."

Mrs. Nkhosi received a call.

"Hallo, Aunty. It's true, Uncle has passed." His voice snuffled from crying.

Mrs. Nkhosi dropped the phone and screamed, her voice reverberating in the house. Tamara received the message of her father's demise within two weeks of her dream.

Author's Notes

This book is based on real-life experiences by the author. The events are real as are the personalities in it – only the names are fictional. She takes the part of Tamara and Anashe, her husband. The lesson in this story is that, when you put God in all you do, He does according to what you ask of him. Jeremiah 33:3 says call unto me, and I will answer thee and show you great and mighty things, which thou knowest not. The prayers of Men are heard by God Almighty if only you believe. When you sincerely pray have faith and believe in God, you have an encounter with Him, He will answer your prayers. God will connect you to people who will help play a certain part in your life. They're called destiny helpers and will take you to your destiny. Tinashe, Fadzai's grandmother, sent her grandson believing that God will be with him wherever he'd go and surely, even if times were hard, he made it and God blessed him.

Anashe was connected to the hardships of his father. He sacrificed for the wellbeing of his family. Fadzai confessed that Anashe's life was a mirror of his life and he released Anashe with the blessing of his grandmother. God's grace was with him to an extent. Whatever he prayed for and requested from God was granted to him in one place. He found a job and a wife at Mr. Nkhosi's home, who knew and worked with his father. God caused Tamara to come into Anashe's life to push him to his destiny. Tamara could hear from God through dreams. God

caused her to have a dream, a vision of the night, so that she could connect to Anashe. Her request was also given to her by connecting her to a man of God who would mentor her and teach her God's ways. She found him in Anashe's pastor. He became her spiritual father. Fadzai broke the ulna bone of his left hand and Anashe also broke the same bone, in different accidents. Fadzai and Anashe both had near death experiences through lion encounters. Anashe's life changed because of God's intervention and direction. Fadzai was still alive at the time of writing this book and was ninety-four years old in 2021. Tamara saw another vision of her father's death, and it was accurate. Mr. Nkhosi (Mr. Simeon Mphanza) passed away on 13th March 2013 at age sixty-five.

"I thank you God for preparing me for my father's death. I moaned him with understanding. God also gave me a chance to anoint and pray for him before his death and I received my blessing. Daddy, may your soul rest in peace."

Our God is an awesome God. He speaks to us so many times. He can even speak to animals and they'd hear Him. He may have spoken to you in many situations, but you ignored Him, or He directs you to a life partner, but because you feel they're not fit for you or are not your class, you deny the direction. You only realise when calamity comes upon you. Let us trust God because He knows us and our destinies. We sometimes seek guidance from Him but refuse it the moment we realise it doesn't please us. I'm grateful to God for connecting me to my husband, Paggie Kandira. If I didn't hear Him and chose another man simply because he was poor, was going to be the time I sealed my doom. Thank you God because…

"YOU DO WONDERS IN MY LIFE"